Pure Creativity

Unleash Your Full Potential

Evy F. Looring

from various sources. Please consult a licensed professional before attempting any techniques outlined in this book.

By reading this document, the reader agrees that under no circumstances is the author responsible for any losses, direct or indirect, that are incurred as a result of the use of the information contained within this document, including, but not limited to, errors, omissions, or inaccuracies.

Table of Contents

Introduction

Albert Einstein once said: "Creativity is intelligence having fun."

How determined are you to learn how to overcome creative blocks and design the most superlative, glorious, and impressive piece of art? Do you want to rank among the likes of Vincent van Gogh, Leonardo da Vinci, Ludwig van Beethoven, and Ernest Hemingway? True creative genius is born in you if you feel a profound urge to express your passions the way these great artists did.

The only problem is that you've hit a brick wall at the speed of light. You find yourself sitting in front of a blank canvas, unable to piece ideas together to create an image never seen before. You yearn to paint something that catches the eye of people who appreciate your expression, but nothing's coming out. Maybe you're a writer who's itching to tap away at the keyboard, but there's nothing to direct your fingers.

The idea of becoming an unstoppable, unmatchable creative is your deepest desire, but your mind doesn't want to follow through with the plan. The disappointment is soul-wrenching, and the fear of uncertainty in the art world makes your stomach clench tight. It doesn't help that your loved ones are also telling you to forget about a career in art because you can't be van Gogh or Hemingway.

This hurts you even further and you fall deeper into the well of invisible ideas. The harder you try to put words together or stroke your brush across the canvas, the deeper you sink into the quagmire of a mental block. You've tried everything and you can't understand how you can be experiencing this block after creating work that stunned people before. Your mind seems lost in this well, even though ideas are close enough to touch.

It doesn't matter what your medium is, the truth is that most of us hit a brick wall from time to time. Writers, painters, sculptors, musicians, composers, and photographers fall into the pits of lost ideas and distant inspiration. Calligraphers, designers, actors, and illustrators aren't immune to the stagnancy of creative genius either. Creativity is misunderstood as a constant flow of ingenuity and wow moments.

Every artist reaches a point where they can't put their ideas together to create something new, unique, and original enough to wow the world. It also doesn't help that the words "struggling artist" are echoed throughout the world as stereotypical.

Creativity is misconstrued in so many ways. Artists aren't the only creative geniuses that walk this earth, because they aren't the only people who passionately desire to create something that astonishes everyone.

Scientists are also creative geniuses, for example, Albert Einstein could never have achieved what he did if he had no passion and ingenuity. The world would still be in the dark ages. Artists, scientists and other creative people have played a big role in history.

There are so many names that carry value hundreds of years later, and their value only seems to snowball into bigger numbers. However, true creatives see past the monetary value as they look into the window of the artists' passions to see how they've not only created history, but their ideas also evolved to advance the world as we know it today. The western world was pretty bland until the Art Nouveau Period between 1890 and 1910.

Creative geniuses chose to emphasize natural curves and use the beauty of nature to inspire elegant decor and furniture. It was all about asymmetry combined with curves to design new splendor, with iron, ceramics, and glass used to beautify the creations. Suddenly, the world became more colorful as it contained a certain *je ne sais quoi* that showed how the essence of life flowed through architecture and decor.

The Art Nouveau period was sparked by artists, but it created an avalanche of periodic design and decor that would still be popular a century later. Creativity is found in every corner of the world, under every stone, and behind every curtain. This doesn't mean that you won't hit a brick wall, but it means that you can break through it with some help.

Think about the common term "writer's block." Writers don't actually suffer from the inability to write a story per se, but they suffer from a creative block. Creation blocks are the consequence of not being able to format words in your mind because your internal dialogue needs to piece words together from multiple inspirational ideas to create one new idea for a painting, sculpture, or illustration (Sapiurka, 2015). It isn't as simple as not being able to draw a picture or write a story.

Every idea, picture, photograph, or novel is a collection of words that the brain must piece together, and a creative block happens when the language collective battles to define a new idea. This can be caused by internal and external factors that contribute to blocking your flow of ideas. Your mind and the environment might be flowing against you, and all you need is to reconnect with the flow to find your words and inspiration again.

Creativity is far more valuable than monetary appreciation. The National Assembly of State Arts Agencies (NASAA) released statistics to prove that creativity and genius are the forerunners of the economy (NASAA, 2015). In fact, arts and cultural production amounted to an astronomical $877 billion or 4.5% of the country's gross domestic product (GDP) output in 2017. Creativity, art, and ingenuity are highly desirable in the workforce.

More than half of the creative geniuses in the United States (US) are employed in the private sector, but being creative makes you 3.6 times more likely to become an entrepreneur. This is good news, as I'm sure you've established your private studio already. Don't fret if you haven't because you stand a higher chance than someone who isn't creative. Your creativity is more valuable than you think.

That's because creative types are capable of higher intelligence, better problem-solving, and originality in its true form. You have what others wish to possess. That doesn't stop mental blocks from challenging you, though. Look at the numbers of creative geniuses in the workforce and tell me that they don't hit brick walls frequently. The fact that your creative brain is so valuable means that internal reasons for blocks must be diminished.

Your desires and passions also rely on the ability to form words and ideas in your mind. You can't be unstoppable if you're not focusing on all the factors that contribute to your ingenuity. Art is a source of income, but it's also more than that. It evolves us and rewards our deepest desires. Whether you're trying to prevent mental blocks from happening for monetary reasons or you want to lead a fulfilling life, you need to learn how to stop mental blocks from lasting for eons.

I was once just as frustrated as you. My passion for writing and drawing has always been a part of me, but there were times I didn't know how to express myself. My deepest wish is to paint the world with my poetry, but sometimes, I can't find the words and instead, use charcoal to illustrate the ideas in my mind. I never gave up, though. I hate the "struggling artist" fallacy spread by people who don't understand creative genius.

I've made a living from my creativity for the last two decades, and it's come with its ups and downs. My bumpy road wasn't the only one as I worked alongside some of the most creative people the world has to offer. I collected tricks and techniques that help me overcome my mental blocks every time, without fail. I've reached a stage where I can spark creativity on command and I've mastered my title.

My insane database of tricks has landed me a six-figure income by living solely from my passion, expressions, and creativity. It breaks my heart to see artists battle for inspiration. It tears me apart to watch creatives give their dreams up because they listen to the hum of loved ones telling them to stop wasting their time, or they don't see any value in their own work when they realize how massive the art world is.

The beauty is that there's room for every artist to express their deepest passions and give people a window into their souls. No one has ever become overwhelmed by art. It's not something we can ever get sick of, on the contrary, it's something everyone craves. Just as you crave expression and inspiration, so does the next person. Your work could light their way to their own creations and spark compounding inspiration.

I've created this guide to help you tap into the creative genius inside of you. You'll welcome the most passionate and ingenious person into your forefront to help you express the desires that burn inside of you. I share the brain's role in creativity and how you can stop your mental blocks from happening internally. You'll always find words to express something, even if it isn't what you originally wanted.

Sometimes, we find better ventures and create more astonishing work when we harness the power of our brains. Intelligence and creativity are intertwined like oxygen and life. You'll learn the 20 secrets of becoming unstoppable in your ingenuity. You have what it takes, but you must possess it like the demon possesses the child in *The Exorcist*. You'll embody everything you need and even learn to tap into your environment.

The world is filled with endless inspiration and it can help you translate your thoughts into amazing ideas. Ancient practices have become popular in western cultures because the evidence of their efficiency is undeniable. Who knew that it was so simple to harness these creation environments? Who knew that you can activate your creative genius on command with 20 tricks?

The creative spark flows through everything that exists, and sometimes, you simply need to call upon it without effort. Every technique, trick, and secret in this book brings you one step closer to breaking free from the chains on your ingenious mind. Don't stop now, never give up, and dedicate yourself to the simplicity of the information in this book to become the greatest you.

If you want to reach the ranks of the most famous artists in the world, you must seek more and continue to Chapter One.

Chapter 1:

Tapping Into Your Truth

Artists of every kind have much in common. On one hand, their ultimate desire in life is to design, create, write, or photograph something incredibly unique that showcases their individuality. On the other hand, artists also use their creative pursuits to earn a living, and they need people to love their creation as much as they do. This paradox is often why creative types hit a brick wall. How can you express your unique artistry while pleasing other people to make money from it?

The answer lies within your inner truth, and that's what we'll focus on first. The embodiment and expression of your true self is how you turn your individuality into inspiration and joy for the people around you without you needing to sacrifice your passions. We'll be getting into mind hacks and techniques to master your ingenuity, but for now, you'll learn about the most important aspect of your creativity.

Beware the Pitfall

Being creative isn't only about being comfortable with your passion. It's also about being connected to your true self. Creative genius is merely an expression of your inner truth. Sadly, the world is filled with diseased ideation. Normopathy is a condition where we have a deep desire to please everyone and blend into society. We want to be accepted as normal in a perfectly abnormal world. You aren't a chameleon that must blend into the background of society. Your individuality is what makes you valuable for reasons better than being loved by the next person.

Normopathy prevents you from being the best version of yourself because you're adapting to the world. You have this deep fear of rejection. This isn't a new crisis either. It's been around for a long time, but it keeps showing its ghastly face. People have always felt the need to conform to societal trends and rules. This can be good when it comes to abiding by the law, but it isn't conducive to creative souls. Technology has amplified the evidence of normopathy in our lives. Harvard professor Howard Gardner, and teacher Katie Davis, saw how technology was worsening the condition and diminishing creativity in students (DiMaria, 2015).

They developed a new theory called "app mentality," where they could see how students were navigating their lives in the same way that they would with their smartphone applications. Every time a new app hits the market, every student must have it, or they won't fit in with the crowd. It didn't matter if their phones were outdated because they'd simply upgrade their devices. This is a sad reality, but it can be seen on social media too. Online challenges are one example where one person posts the most ridiculous exercise, and everyone else follows like sheep.

It's understandable for challenges like the amyotrophic lateral sclerosis (ALS) ice bucket challenge, in 2014, because it was for a good cause. Challengers had to dowse themselves in a bucket of ice water and post it online. Unfortunately, there have been highly questionable challenges too. For example, the eating/swallowing of Tide pods.

Nevertheless, everyone wants to fit in, no matter how dangerous it is. The problem is that we become desensitized to stupidity just as we do to violence. I don't call these challenges creative because it encourages sheep mentality where you follow the masses and gain a few giggles. Sheep mentality prevents our true selves from creating genuine art. Trying to fit into a world of individuals will lead to emotional suffering from your side. You'll be disappointed, frustrated, and feel like a failure.

Most of humankind suffers from sheep mentality, but they don't like other sheep. You can't explore who you really are if you're following the herd. You'll fail creatively if you try to please every person in your life, including those who pay money to enjoy your artwork.

First, you'll attract fewer people because they'll assume that you're weak. Strength is shown by someone who isn't afraid of being themselves. The type of people you want in your life don't like people-pleasers. Strong people might be polite with you but they want to be with their own kind.

One of the biggest fears that drive the sheep mentality is that we dread rejection. Everyone wants to be part of something and rejection is as painful as a knife through your heart. Unfortunately, the people you're trying to please and gain admiration and respect from will eventually reject you, and this pain is indescribable. Sadly, you'll up your game to please them even more and end up being rejected even harder. Your idea of who you should be, and who you pretend to be, grows so distant that you resent yourself.

You'll even become resentful towards friends and family because they don't treat you respectfully. It's understandable to feel like you're being manipulated and used, but the truth is far more painful than that. You've been conditioning them to treat you a certain way and therefore, you've manipulated them first. Yes, they're manipulating you now, but it's because you've conditioned them.

Moreover, even those closest to you will stop trusting you. Your friends and family will see you as an agreeable person who always tells them what they want to hear. Failure to speak your mind will only make people trust you less because they're not sure if you're sincere or not. Losing people's trust will decrease your confidence because they won't confide in you anymore.

Ironically, the fear of rejection will lead to lost friends, companions, and inspirational mentors. Life is a funny concept because those we want acceptance from are the very people who disappear. People might not outright reject you but you're untrustworthy and weak in their hearts.

Your desire to please everyone also becomes a double-edged sword when you have two friends who don't agree on something. How do you please one side without upsetting the other one? The friendship between them can become untethered, and you're left to choose sides.

Your resentment will grow for the people you try to satisfy. For example, you're known as the go-to videographer for social events. Your friends and colleagues will always come to you, but you won't know whether they truly value you, or if they simply use your freely given skills. You could start resenting what you once loved too. Videography is a creative art form, but when your friends constantly ask you to be the cameraman, you won't enjoy the experience anymore. You'll resent your artistry because you're behind the camera at all the memorable events.

Making everyone else happy comes back to bite you. You're unhappy in this situation. You can't cater to your passions, and do the same for every person around you. They might also have a sheep mentality, but they pretend to take pride in their individuality. I can't agree more with the phrase that you can't make everyone happy, but you sure can enrage everyone.

The only way you can hone your inner truth is to realize that you can't please everyone. You're an individual with skills, strengths, creativity, and passions of your own. Free yourself from the sheep mentality disease by finding out who you are. Failing to be true to yourself is a lesson often learned the hard way. Every creative person stumbles at some point, but moving away from the herd is how you start regaining your ideas and sharing them with the people who enjoy them.

Individual Inspiration

There's one secret to creative truth. Everyone speaks about originality, but you can simply use an old idea that everyone forgot about, and make it new. Move away from the herd, but watch them and gain inspiration from them. You're not trying to be accepted back into the herd, but rather, you are expressing your individuality by using inspiration to create something with your vision. The ideas of *new* and *original* are more complicated than you think. Artists need to be unique, but the word original mustn't be misunderstood either. It doesn't mean that you must fathom ideas from nothing.

It means that you take inspiration and put your unique twist on it. A painter doesn't design an image from nothing. He has a collection of creative ideas stimulated by sensory input from the world, and this explodes onto a canvas of individuality. You don't need to sit in front of a tree and paint it, but your ideas come from fragments of inspiration in memory. Therefore, you're welcome to gather inspiration from other artists as any writer, painter, and photographer does, but you need to add the twist that makes it yours.

This personal twist will be guided by your inner truth, but people, places, and objects will ignite the idea you concoct. Browse the internet for random ideas and piece them together to allow inspiration to flow. Other people might not see the connection between the ideas, but you can make them see it. Abstract art is a risky business, and it only works if you can make people connect the dots they've never seen before. Suddenly, the artwork becomes original. The inspiration for this concoction will be unique and showcases your perception of the world. As much as we'd like to deny it, art is stolen. Inspiration is stolen.

The secret to owning your artwork is to allow yourself to be distantly inspired by others and the environment, and then let your work inspire those around you. You can guarantee the two-way street of inspiration with five simple rules.

First, surround yourself with like-minded people. Everyone will be different, but they'll have a few things in common. Share your passion for creating new concepts with people who do the same. Nothing's stopping you from asking them questions either. Allow them to inspire you and offer them the same benefits. Gaining inspiration isn't being a sheep. Listen to the stories from people who've been in a rut before and how they overcame it. Adopt a mentor to help you be yourself and burst with inspiration.

Your responsibility to them would be to remain authentic, which is the second rule. Don't give them any less than what they offer. Being authentic is what inspires other people. Allow your inner freak to come out if this is who you truly are. If you've surrounded yourself with like-minded people, they'll understand. They might even show their own freakiness. Tell them stories, be open and vulnerable, and share your failures with them. You can inspire people by showing them your battle scars.

Rule number three says that you must make sure your like-minded people are challenging you to excel at greater things. Showing someone how to succeed is the most inspirational spark you can ignite. Allow your creative crowd to have high expectations of you because you'll be driven to achieve them. Don't be afraid to ask for advice, and follow someone great.

Rule number four is to remain positive. Being positive can work for you and the person you're gaining inspiration from. Positivity encourages inspiration and motivation. Only use constructive criticism to convey your inner truth to your friends. Listen to their constructive opinions when they return the favor too.

Inspiring people build us up instead of breaking us down. We want them to be supportive and enthusiastic with us.

The fifth rule says that we must be spontaneous and change things up. Sometimes, our current crowd can't inspire us, and neither can our surroundings. This is why creative people shake things up frequently. Exit your comfort zone and allow your inner explorer to learn new things, experience new excitements, and find inspiration in new places. Leave your garage and paint in the park for the day. Take a break when you need to and walk along the warm beach sand to find new inspiration

Erasing your sheep mentality, honing your inner truth, and being the distant wolf that watches the herd and environment for inspiration is how you start opening your mind to the possibilities of creativity. I call you a wolf, but as you can see by the five rules, there's no harm intended towards other people. Wolves have a keen sense of awareness, and they're patient animals that stalk the herd. You aren't stalking the herd or scanning the environment for negative reasons. You're collecting inspiration from the sheep and the environment as you watch from far away. Remember that wolves are also pack animals, so never forget to surround yourself with inspirational wolves.

Tapping Your Truth

Getting to know yourself, your desires, and your needs is hard for many people. You need to learn how to tap into your truth so that it is reborn to the world again. The only thing original in this world is the truth that lies deep within you. Who are you at your deepest core? There are a few ways we can tap into ourselves to learn who we are because the hardest part of being inauthentic is living a life that isn't satisfying.

As with anything in life, start at the beginning. Dig into your roots and learn about your ancestors to see who they were. Many characteristics are genetic, and knowing who your ancestors were could help you expose inner strengths. Take a hereditary deoxyribonucleic acid (DNA) test to see where your culture found its roots. Learn more about the values and beliefs of your ethnic culture with some research.

Individualism has also been wrongly shadowed in modernism, but knowing your true self is something you can express in your creativity. Many people fear their inner truths, or they deny that they have certain values or talents. There's nothing to be ashamed of when it comes to your differences. Your uniqueness is a value in this world because it leads to your purpose. A life without purpose isn't one worth living. Learn to accept who you are and love the value you bring.

This leads to another way of being true to yourself. Don't be afraid to pursue dreams and desires because you think you'll be judged for your differences. Your happiness needn't be sacrificed for anyone. Do what you love and break out in dance when music plays if this is your passion. Create the most beautiful sketches if you love drawing. Your happiness is dependent on your ability to give your deeper desires an expression. Be the person who leaves a boring life behind to pursue the art world even if you've already had a few ruts.

Being honest with yourself is another way to learn about your core. Don't be afraid to be open, vulnerable, and curious with yourself. Being honest with other people might be a challenge at first, but you'll overcome it once you realize how much people value you for your uniqueness. Being honest with yourself, however, is a more complicated rule. You might need to focus on learning to love your talents, differences, and oddities again to make sure you don't fear being vulnerable to the only person that matters—you.

Introspection is an amazing journey to look beyond the daily rat race, your physical being, and the emotions that move in and out of your life. The true self is an invisible part of you that tells you who you are and what your purpose is. It encumbers every part of your life, passions, environment, mentality, physical being, emotional grounding, and the community. The hard truth is that no one lives in their true shell all the time. It's okay if you occasionally slip backward while learning to know yourself.

One method to overcome the idea that you need to be perfect at all times is by understanding and accepting that things can look different to everyone. The way you defeat the chance of allowing this to deter you from being your true self is to learn to see things from various perspectives. That's why I say that the wolf watches from a distance. He sees all and watches everyone because no two people experience an event the same way. You can use a light exercise to determine how everyone views things differently.

Stand face to face with someone in a room. Determine which side of the room is the left and right sides. Your opinions will differ because you're standing in varying places. Think about the places being circumstances in life. The fact remains that both persons are right when they have opposing opinions about which side of the room is the left side. They're looking at things from different viewpoints and won't be able to agree unless they were facing the same direction. Their current positions, including all the circumstances around them, are determining their reality at any time. This is how your reality is formed and that's why you need to look closer at your inner self.

Your views and passions differ from other people, but this is what makes you unique. Yes, you can learn to see things from other people's perspectives, but you should never allow your truth to be shadowed by them. Start by learning to meditate on your inner truth. Just relax and allow your body, emotions, thoughts, and viewpoints to surface for acknowledgment. You're not correcting them or arguing against them.

You want to learn what they are and how they developed. The inner self is thought to be your soul, heart, or deepest truth. Notice whether your mind or heart pay attention to the feelings in your body because this shows whether your truth is guiding you. You want your heart to recognize the circumstances in your body and environment. You don't want your mind to control this introspection alone.

The final method for knowing who you are is to recognize what you want. Ask yourself a few questions and remember to answer them from your heart.

First, what is it that you yearn for? For example, I want to buy a house with the income I earn from my creative talents.

Secondly, what experience do you wish to achieve? I want to experience abundant earnings to make my dream come true and ensure that my needs are met.

Thirdly, how would you achieve this? I'll teach myself to find inspiration in everything by following the exercises in this book. Once inspiration hits me, I can work on my multiple masterpieces to get to my goal.

Keep asking yourself these three questions to develop your true self. Your ultimate desires are normally highlighted by your truth.

Inner Confidence

Know this - not everyone will love the real you and that's okay. Your truth won't shine the light in every corner of your life, but who cares as long as it lights the way to success. It's easy to be wary of your true self when it feels like a stranger, but you can learn to become confident to express it. Self-doubt has a sneaky way of entering your mind when your heart is trying to lead. Use confidence to allow the mind to calm down and give way to the heart.

When you're feeling uncertain about being yourself, your first tool is to remind yourself of a time you felt amazingly confident. Maybe you showed a new flair that expressed your truth with friends last week when you wore a new outfit. Remind yourself of how your confidence has worked for you in the past.

Confidence is a funny thing because you can also trick your mind into believing that you're ready for whatever comes. Dubbed as *power poses* in 2012, Amy Cuddy exposed the powerful influence posture can have on our confidence (Booth, 2018). Sit straight and push those shoulders back to assert confidence and trick your mind into believing it.

Otherwise, give yourself some positive confirmation by affirming your qualities out loud. Stand in front of your reflection and use positive affirmations to tell yourself why you're great, what you can do, and what your strengths are. Saying "you've got this" is mighty influential to the brain.

Confidence is also a choice if you commit to thinking positively about yourself. Don't run yourself down and don't give other people the chance to do it either. Maintaining positive vibes about yourself, and removing negative naysayers from your life, help you to walk tall.

Being self-confident is one thing, but you'll encounter some negative feelings when other people criticize you. Everyone has a different reality and you'll be exposed to some negative feedback infrequently. Accept the person's opinion as theirs, use inspiration from constructive criticism, and move beyond the negative feelings that criticism brings.

Make yourself feel good on the outside and your insides will thank you. Wear something amazing, do your hair up, or have a makeover. Keep a few power boosts around for when your confidence is low. Your brain knows that you see yourself as gorgeous in that red dress or with a certain shade of lipstick.

Also, don't be hard on yourself when you have a bad day. We all experience unwanted days and shouldn't allow them to deter our confidence. Rather, be compassionate and give yourself some time to overcome the emotions.

Self-limiting beliefs can also hold your confidence hostage. Don't allow past opinions or failures to limit your mind. Your teacher might have called you a creative dead zone, but she wasn't the most inspirational mentor, and you know what they say. Sometimes, those who can't create art are those who teach it. Introspection isn't always enough to overcome limiting thoughts. Exposure to the things you fear and succeeding at what you never imagined is how you move past this problem. Start experimenting with new experiences.

That reminds me that you shouldn't allow false memories to control your confidence either. Memories aren't always trustworthy. The mind works with a negative bias and your brain will remind you of everything bad about an experience (Quy, 2016). This is especially true if you've been hiding from your truth for a long time. Your confirmation bias picks up all the negative beliefs you've held over yourself. Memory and facts must be divided to make sure your confidence stays around. Remember that your reality is merely a single perspective.

Curiosity is another key to open the boundless world of inner confidence. Do you know why investigators are good at their job? They allow their perspective to change to see all the contributing factors. Curiosity and imagination can lay new pathways for you. We remain teachable as long as our curiosity is alive, and we need to be willing to absorb lessons and stimulus to be inspired.

Finally, grow comfortable with yourself because trying to make everyone like you is the downfall of confidence when you're trying to be true to yourself. We all have haters but don't allow this to erase your confidence. Your uniqueness will make some people love you and others might be repelled by it. You shouldn't have to be anyone but yourself to experience genuine relationships. It's also fine to feel sad if some people don't like the real you. You're an emotional creature and shouldn't suppress your feelings. Losing people that we care about can be so emotional that it causes physical pain (Fishbein, n.d.). Don't blame yourself for people walking away because it's their loss and not your burden to carry.

The most painful breakups happen between romantic partners. Know that it's not your fault if someone steers away from you. Never allow yourself to question your worth because someone else couldn't handle the amazing person inside of you. They were once in love with the fake you and how much longer did you want to maintain the falsities? Not everyone is compatible, and some people just can't handle the heat. By heat, I mean that you're smoking hot with your talents and creative genius. Just make sure that your behavior never reaches arrogant levels.

Being too confident will send everyone packing. Losing someone who disliked your true self is one thing, but look for patterns where even your new friends are vanishing. This indicates that you're too confident. There's no word to describe an unbalanced and overly confident person better than arrogant. Be confident but steer clear of arrogance.

Against All Odds

Forgetting about everyone's opinions and perceptions can be hard, but you must dismiss criticism that pulls you further away from your true self. Take things with a grain of salt when someone offends you, and only use self-growth information if it's constructive. Never allow your true self to waver with the world's different opinions. Learn to live in a world that doesn't always agree with your truth.

You can't live a fulfilling life when you're surrounded by fabrication, dishonesty, denial, and misinterpretations. The problem is that many of us build our truths on societal dysfunction in our childhoods. Our roles served others and not ourselves. Even today, kids learn to live by and conform to the societal rules. They don't learn to set their own values or question anything. Growing up gives you the power to erase this fallacy from your mind and set your truth. If you continue to allow other people to define you, you'll remain as far from your inner truth as you can be, and you won't find true fulfillment.

Stop trying to impress the world because you can't meet their standards by being fake. For those who think you're missing the point, they can find someone else to conform to their version of reality. What you choose to live with as an adult, will be what you choose to learn, and what is ultimately practiced in your life. You know that your reality differs from everyone else's, so flourish in your own views, values, and choices. Being yourself and balancing your expressions can be achieved without harming those around you too. Being authentic doesn't mean that you must resonate with the untruths that built your confirmation bias in the first place. You're going to make enemies if you tell the whole truth all of the time.

Choose your battles, I'm sure your sister doesn't like hearing how much weight she's gained, and your friend hates the constant truth about how you feel about her idiotic boyfriend. You don't have to tell the whole truth every time because you'll find it hard to survive in a world with sheep if you do. Instead, speaking your truth should be saved for moments where it's needed. You mustn't speak either if you don't believe it to be true. Is your sister's weight hurting you? Then it might be time to discuss it with her once and not nag her. Tell her how you truthfully fear for her health. You don't want to see her unhappy and only mention the real reasons for your discussion.

Setting clear boundaries can also prevent relationship problems with people who differ in opinion. So, they believe that paintings can't earn a living unless you're van Gogh, but your opinion is different because you've seen the fruits of your labor. Let people know that your boundaries are firm when it comes to your artwork. Communicating clearly with people allows them to know where you're negotiable and where you aren't. Just know that you must respect their boundaries too.

Some people avoid their truth because they fear what others might think. This happens often with authority figures or people who are important to us. They bring an idea to us that they think is the next masterful plan for wealth or it might be something to solve a problem. Don't be scared to tell them the logic you see, and they've missed. Chances are that many authority figures, such as bosses will be more experienced or knowledgeable than us, but there might be a time that we know more. Avoid arrogance and share your opinion because they'll respect you for showing them the genuine flaws in their plan.

Withholding your truth has consequences for you and the people around you. You lose authenticity every time you choose to keep quiet. You're choosing your battles but rather say nothing if you're going to echo someone else's truth. Creativity and inspiration lie below intelligently contributing to the community, and avoiding the truth can prevent you from harnessing this gift.

Instead, make open communication your second nature and speak your truth while encouraging people around you to follow with open communication. Own up to mistakes too and listen to someone else's opinion. You might see a better opportunity in their viewpoint. Open communication also means that you must recognize that everyone has their opinions. Encourage them to speak their truth and share insights with them. This could lead to double-sided inspiration again. Listen to everyone with an open heart because you get to choose what you believe.

Open communication must contain assertiveness to make your boundaries effective as well. Your communication with anyone must possess five aspects.

- Be specific about what happened and skip no details. Tell the person what exactly upset you because an incomplete picture is a dangerous start.
- Secondly, share your feelings in detail with them. Their actions made you feel so-and-so.
- Thirdly, explain what you'd like to experience in the future. Never be judgmental but suggest a solution that benefits both of you.
- Fourthly, offer the person some actionable steps that they can take to prevent the problem from happening again. Be calm about this and tell them, for example: "I'd like you to call me before arriving to make sure I'm available."
- Finally, ask them what they think about your suggestions.

Look, the world's going to go on when you expose your truth. The best you can do is adapt and commit to being honest with yourself and other people. There's no need to be arrogant or hurtful either. Solutions are often found when two heads become one. However, you don't need to sacrifice your truth if the relationship isn't conducive anymore. Express yourself as artists should. Be you, and allow the world to either love or hate you.

Knowing That You've Strayed

You can stray from your truth even after being honest with yourself. A few signs can help you recognize whether you've derailed from the goal.

Not standing in your truth, loving and being kind to yourself, and living an authentic life can be seen when you start shying away from public events, especially those that would benefit you. Shyness is a sign that you're not comfortable with yourself anymore.

Asking other people what they think is another worrisome sign. The hesitation or doubt that creeps up on you when you're supposed to say something is a backslide.

The fear of conflict is another problem because you'll love yourself enough to stop fearing different opinions if you're true to yourself.

Watch out for signs that you used to show as well. Going with the flow and agreeing with everyone indicates that you've lost touch with your truth again.

You might've strayed when you find yourself only sticking to people with the same opinions as you again. Yes, you want a like-minded group, but you also need to challenge yourself and feel comfortable enough to stand for your truth in the face of differential thinking. You can't be unique in a pool of chameleons.

Sometimes, we can also express our inner complexities onto other people. Do you judge others for being different from you? This indicates that you can't accept your uniqueness and it's a sign that you're off track too.

Wanting to be perfect all the time can also indicate you have strayed. Being comfortable with your truth means that you accept all your imperfections as well. You won't judge your weaknesses unless you've forgotten your truth.

An obvious sign of backsliding is when someone can't accept criticism. Remember that being true to yourself means that you must sift through criticism and use what you can while disposing of what you find harmful.

Finally, are you doubting yourself when you say no now? This shows that you aren't confident to assert your boundaries anymore. Be sincere every time you say no.

Don't allow a backslide to get you down and rather commit to accepting and harnessing your truth again.

Grounding Unshakable Truth

Understand that first, they laugh when you make waves, then they ridicule, and finally, they'll ask you how you did it. Your most precious creativity will flourish when you hold nothing back and allow your truth to stand tall. Honest expressions catalyze creative mastery. Once your truth is mastered and you allow your thoughts and emotions to flow freely without restrictions and muzzles, you'll find your creative genius. It's undeniably priceless to tap into your truth and ground yourself in its solid foundation before you apply any of the other techniques in this book.

Start by taking responsibility for your happiness because you can lead a fulfilling life if you step up to the plate. Don't wait for happiness from other people. Be sure to remove toxic, negative, and judgmental people because you can't ground yourself if you're surrounded by toxicity. Spend time getting to know yourself with introspection. Keep a journal about your feelings, thoughts, and experiences to learn more about what makes you tick. Allocate a time every day for introspection, otherwise, you'll be forgetting to do it.

Activate your heart by using relaxation techniques and become aware of how the heart and mind need to work together. Everyone claims that we must only use our minds to lead us, but that's a lie. We need our hearts to guide our true selves. Pranayama breathing exercises, yoga, Reiki healing, guided meditation, and mindfulness will help you open your heart to your true self. Be compassionate, caring, and kind to yourself so that you don't depend on people liking you. Accepting yourself is part of being mindful and creating your own future. Fate is only what you make it.

Never forget to be open with yourself, so don't repress emotions. Bring them to the surface with guided meditation and learn to acknowledge them. The longer you focus on emotions and the way they make your physical body, heart, and mind feel, the more they dissipate over time. Forgiveness and letting go are also methods of self-acceptance. Don't hold a grudge against yourself and move past mistakes. We all make them and it doesn't weaken your truth. Remove the anger you feel towards yourself when you stumbled in your meditation sessions by allowing the feelings to dissipate.

Gain new respect for yourself by choosing boundaries you won't negotiate. Make them known to your social and workgroups and try your best not to forget them. You can't love yourself if you don't respect yourself. One boundary we can all benefit from is learning to say no. Don't just say it either. Be assertive and walk away calmly when you say no. Allow yourself to connect deeply with those who respect your lifestyle and creativity. Everyone needs to be connected to people and this helps us build a support group for when times are tough too. Your support group can be a grounded foundation in your life if you surround yourself with the right people.

Root yourself to customs, rituals, and routines to further strengthen your truth. Life seems so much simpler when we know what to expect and create customs that we love. Don't rely on the current family and friends' rituals alone. Creating personally customized rituals makes it more meaningful to you. It can be as simple as having a dinner party every Thursday or joining a spiritual group that hikes up mountains every month. Open your eyes wide and give yourself reasons to be you. Moreover, add daily rituals that promote mindfulness. Use distraction exercises to guide your senses through a morning routine. I'd sit in my garden and listen, smell, see, feel, and taste the nature that envelops me.

Your daily ritual could include controlled breathing where you count the intake of air and press it out for the same amount of time. Even journaling is a mindful ritual, but allow yourself to have sociable and solitary rituals you can practice daily. You can also ground yourself with humor. It's part of being gentle and kind to yourself. Laughter is a great experience, and it creates such a peaceful space around you. Forget about troubles and make other people laugh with you. Begin a ritual with a friend where you share a joke every morning before the craze of life kicks in. You send them a joke today and tomorrow they must return the favor. Not only will you be giggling every morning, but you'll be reading a lot of funny stuff as you look for your next joke.

Finally, promise yourself that you'll dare to dream. This is crucial for someone who must be true to themselves and ground themselves daily. Guided meditation sessions can help you dream big and imagine the greatest future. It also sparks creativity as a bonus. Commit to learning how to meditate freely by following a few guided sessions first. If you make mistakes, move on from them. If you create a new masterpiece, congratulate yourself and allow your true self to be recognized for what you achieved.

Finding your inner truth and honing it is where you begin your journey to creative genius. It might sound complicated but all you need is to believe in yourself and dedicate yourself to the truth that lives inside of you.

Chapter 2:

The Responding Brain

Creativity and science are not opposing entities as some people might believe. In fact, creativity is in many ways a byproduct of neurological functions in the brain. Your heart is the soul of your truth, but caring for and enhancing the brain is conducive to your creative genius. The human brain is an artistic creation in its own right, and you'll briefly learn how to use the brain's response to ignite the spark of ingenuity.

Understanding Creativeness

Creativity is a part of every person since it involves someone taking an existing idea and transforming it into a new one. It's a dream or imagined idea that we turn into reality because our dreams collect information from inspired memories and transform them into an understandable concept. You can also think of creativity as finding a solution to a problem, much like innovation. People who deny their creativity, or don't want to be thought of as a child, will have varying definitions of creativity and innovation. Believe it or not, they're the same thing.

Innovation is what adults call creativity once they're older. Children are the most creative beings, and some of us are fortunate enough to never forget our inner child. Children play and learn daily by using their imagination. We encourage our kids to reach for the stars, but sadly, we tell ourselves that adults must be realistic. However, children are at their most creative essence during early childhood development because they rely on their innocence, curiosity, playfulness, and basic instincts to learn. They don't know anything yet, but they have a deep urge to survive in this big new world.

The only way they can learn to do all the things we take for granted is by making mistakes, testing environmental boundaries, and pushing themselves further. Early childhood is a flurry of disobeying the rules because kids aren't limited by adulting. Their minds are free and receptive to everything around them. The more they learn, the less they need to use their creativity to find answers. Most people outgrow childish creativity and think that they must live by society's rules and call themselves inventive innovators instead. This is the wrong way of looking at creativity, no matter who tells you to grow up.

Some of the greatest minds in art and science have never allowed their inner child to grow up. Albert Einstein was intelligently ingenious, but Picasso and Mozart were just as creatively intelligent. They all saw an idea that's come from somewhere and transformed it into inventions to make life simpler, or art that brought us closer to true happiness. Industrialization has also tried to kill creativity, but inventors, engineers, and even mathematicians are creative geniuses. They took something that wasn't good enough yet and connected the dots that no one else could.

Here is a simple example to understand how adult innovation has peaked through industrialism. Landlines were invented to help people communicate with each other until some brilliant person decided to up the game. Why should we only be able to communicate with loved ones from our homes? The mobile phone was born and it was closely followed by the miniature computer we call smartphones today. Creativity is an inborn trait we all possess, but we must exercise it instead of giving into negative notions about it. Yes, it comes with embarrassment at times.

Sure, it can make people call you a child. However, using it is how you become the best version of yourself. You'll always look for more answers. Creativity is sparked whenever you need to solve a problem, find a new way of doing things, or to stop being a sheep. It's ignited by anyone who questions the status quo, themselves, or the rules set by other people. It can be instigated and honed through socializing, playfulness, and having a keen eagerness to improve an existing idea. Creativity is what makes your artwork stand out from the ocean available, but it should never be restricted to leisure ideations alone.

You use your creativity daily, every time you overcome the tiniest obstacles. Do you want to plan a birthday party? Well, it would be dreary and repulsive to guests if you didn't give it some creative thought first. You have to tap into your inner child to create a memorable experience. Everyone wants the party of the century and it won't happen without your creative genius. Millennials are showing more creativity by the day because it's become a trend to be yourself and stand out from the crowd. We often see the most ridiculous fashion statements and art that make us squint.

However, they've used their creative power to show you something that connects the dots of the unseen. Moreover, creativity gives us a purpose and is called the origin of true happiness. The secret to happiness lies within the ability to create something that makes your internal music flow. Think of a pianist as the music ebbs and flows throughout his body, mind, and soul. He becomes so lost in his music that he detaches himself from the environment and his physical being.

Becoming this intertwined with your creativity by doing something you love is like learning the art of the deepest transcendental meditation. You leave the presence you're in and don't feel pain and sadness. The music carries the pianists' soul to another plane, and he gets lost in a deeper purpose. Your subconscious mind and heart blend into a perfect duo to carry your ideas into an expression of your soul. What could make us happier than finding something worth living for and expressing it purposefully?

Evolutionary and Biological Background

Everyone has creative genius within their DNA, it's only a matter of exercising and mastering it. The Journal of Philosophical Transactions of the Royal Society published multiple scientific facts behind creativity when it comes to evolution (Wiggins et al., 2015). It's known that every living being has one ultimate goal in life—to survive. It's the primal instinct from which everything we've ever done was motivated. A secondary instinct is that we must protect our survival by procreating or creating a footprint of ourselves. Everyone wants to be remembered for something.

Humans aren't the only species with the primal instincts needed to flourish. Animals, such as the blue whale, have also used this instinct to become creative. Blue whales use sounds to communicate their distress and mating requirements, among other reasons. They've learned to alter sounds to attract mates or use a different sound to ward off enemies. Blue whales are also creative artists, but they're just not as evolved as us. Humans have evolved from animals and harnessed the ultimate genius behind creativity to find ways to make life easier, safer, and memorable.

The problem is that we find new challenges as we evolve and need to come up with new ideas to defeat them. The journal shares facts about how the value of creativity has evolved within us. Creativity and value are separate components. We need people to value our creativity to ensure that our footprints remain. Our expectations are always set by history. Michelangelo painted the ceiling of the Sistine Chapel and set the tone for many artists to come. People were shocked and amazed by his creation. Therefore, it stands as an expectation that we compare our murals with. It doesn't mean that we can't improve his work, but it's always a lingering expectation to measure our value against.

Then you have the observers who either feel the connection of your creation, or they don't. Beauty shall always be what the observer perceives it to be. Thirdly, you place a value on your creation, normally by comparing your expectations to history and allocating emotional bondage to the work. The final valuation happens in the circumstances surrounding the observers and yourself at the time of sharing it. For example, Picasso's *Guernica* was painted during the start of what would become the world's greatest war to date. Adolf Hitler was asserting his power and the world was about to fall into dark days.

Picasso was one of the first abstract artists, and he used his creativity to design a painting that wouldn't be understood for years. On the left of the painting was a bull crushing a man's head. The bull represents Hitler and the man was the yet-to-come attempted demise of the Jewish people. Today, the painting is priceless because history was captured, and the world is full of people who find value in this expression, especially because it was created even before we knew what was truly coming. The current circumstances around a piece of art can also add the final value to it. The context in which creation and observation take place can make the difference between a priceless or worthless creation.

In summary, creativity is valued by accounting for the creator, creation, observer, and the circumstances surrounding it. People could connect the dots in Picasso's famous artwork and that's what made it invaluable. Coming back to the evolutionary part of creativity, understand that expectations have so much history to encumber today that it makes people want originality. That's why every artist is striving to bring something new, unheard of, and unseen. Remember that originality doesn't exist, but we've evolved to take inspiration from our ancestors and artists who came before us. Creativity isn't a physical asset, but rather an undying wish to improve something until it stuns people.

The level of improvement isn't always important either, thanks to our hedonic adaptation. This theory means that we want to keep evolving and changing, but we're only capable of doing it slowly. Sometimes, an artist's rendition of an idea is too advanced for the current evolution. Picasso's painting was advanced for the time as Hitler was only stirring trouble. He wasn't the bull depicted in the painting yet. Hedonic adaptation also means that we can't process new information faster than our evolutionary trajectory allows. Our perception can either be novel or so incomprehensible that the new idea carries no value.

Our evolutionary ability to comprehend new ideas can be understood through biology. The University of California (UCLA) focused their attention on the biological side of creativity (Zaidel, 2014). Expressing ourselves through art allows us to reflect our biological needs for survival. The university studied patients with brain damage to see if creativity was one more skill diminished by local injuries. Artistic patients with brain damage showed no less creativity than before having a stroke or ruptured tumor in the brain. Motor skills are commonly erased in stroke patients, but creativity remains.

The biological evidence shows that creativity isn't localized to specific regions in the brain, and you won't lose your talents or skills even if you've suffered trauma. That's the good news, but the even better news is that creativity exists without injury. Our need to survive is a biological default in the brain and is probably the most powerful reason for motivation to create, transform, and invent. Social needs also influence your creative genius, but not as much. Our observation of the world is what creates ideas that ensure our survival and imprint. UCLA describes blue tit birds in England that learned to steal milk from sealed bottles in a desperate means to survive.

However, it was established that social needs also play a role because other blue tit birds learned from the original thieves by observing them and communicating. The community worked together to foil humans because they wanted to live, and they wanted to leave a teachable legacy for their birdy friends. Survival instincts will always help us create new answers, but it's the social needs that drive the communicative expressions in artists. The university also looked at patients with common neurodegenerative conditions to see if their creativity was still awake.

The patients never lost their desire to be social and express their communications so that they can leave a memory behind. Some people say that more intelligent or knowledgeable people create better ideas, but that's only because they have more memories of objects, places, people, skills, goals, ideas, and cultural habits. Increasing your memory and looking for new inspiration is how you start mastering your creativity because it expands your spark of ingenuity. The more you remember, store, and learn, the more you can create.

The Brain on Creative Enhancement

Neuroscience is a dense and complex study of the brain, but it offers us insight and knowledge. Researchers cover the difficult task of connecting a piano key to a specific electrical pulse in the brain. Neurotransmissions are the electrical jolts from one neuron to another that lights our brains up on imaging devices. However, there are billions of these little neurons, and mapping specific pulses requires a patient and brave neuroscientist. To understand their needed persistence better, you must learn that creativity doesn't spark in one tiny section of the brain.

Using our ingenuity can often light the brain up like a sporadic symphony of musicians across the world. You can also think of it as trying to make specific stars brighten more in the vast night sky. It makes sense though because you use more than one region to accomplish the simplest of tasks. Memories are stored throughout the brain and each contains a fragment of information. Therefore, speaking in a full sentence to explain something already requires multiple neurons to activate and send pulses through to each other so that one idea or sequence of words, in this case, are voiced.

Creativity and problem-solving are the same things, so forming a sentence is a creative act. Creativity works in two fashions, though. The first is the flow of information that blends to help us create a new idea or solve a problem. The second process of creativity is the rehearsal or repetition that makes this network stronger. The more each neuron connects to another one, the stronger the connection becomes. There are three functions in your brain that help the pulses along. The executive attention network is what comes to light when you must concentrate or focus on the question or problem. It happens between the prefrontal cortex behind your forehead and the side of your brain known as the parietal lobe.

The executive part of being creative is probably more involved in the repetition of your idea to perfect it. The default network function, better known as the imagination train, constructs mental imagery to simulate the options you have. The imagination stems from the prefrontal cortex as well, but it extends into the parietal and temporal lobes. The images it designs in your vision will use collective data from the neurons sending pulses to create a new image. This is part of the free-flowing creative process. The salience network that resides in the anterior insula and the dorsal anterior cingulate cortices is the final function. It's bombarded with stimulus when you see, hear, feel, taste, and smell things.

It's hard to keep this process focused because it requires deeper concentration. However, this network can help us choose what we want to focus on and what we want to avoid. That gives you an idea of the brain and its regions. It's easy to see why neuroscientists can't pinpoint creativity. The ignition of various regions proves that the brain doesn't have one creative center (Cavdarbasha & Kurczek, 2017). The prefrontal cortex is obviously at work, and it controls short-term and long-term memory. The hippocampus region that lies deeper in the brain is also responsible for storing and regulating memories that hold facts, beliefs, and experiences.

The hippocampus can pull together the neurons that pulse simultaneously and can be used to imagine new ideas. The basal ganglia are one of the deepest parts of the brain, it's much like the soul of the largest organ in your body. These are clusters of neurons that have worked together long enough to form habits and rituals. These clusters also help in decision-making as they scan your memories. Normally, the basal ganglia instruct decisions that are faster than we can stop, such as knowing how to ride a bike or swim once you've learned how to and practiced it enough. This region is important in learning new skills and developing your talents.

White matter is the final key to creativity because it's the very connections through which the pulses travel. Creating stronger connections can help you gather ideas and solutions much easier.

Hidden Brainy Advantages

Latent inhibition sounds like something from a science-fiction movie but it's not that complicated. Everyone is capable of processing stimulation through the senses, and the brain automatically runs the information through the functions we discussed. Most people can shut the constant stream of information intake down at will. Other people can't easily shut the stimulus down. This group of people are known to have a lower-grade of latent inhibition. Being able to process all the intake and still function is quite the challenge though, and is normally more prevalent in higher intelligence.

Having a lower latent inhibition does, however, allow you to process every bit of information, recall fine details through enhanced memory storage, and make you burst with creativity. It leads to creative genius.

Sometimes, people will become overwhelmed with stimulation and need to shut down to stop it. I'm sure you've heard about highly creative types being a little nutty. Harvard researchers wanted to understand why musicians, artists, and writers are at more risk of developing mental disorders (Eby, 2020).

The results showed that intelligence and creativity can coexist easily, but having high latent inhibitors can cause neurological dysfunction. These people's brains quickly sift through information and block out anything they deem unnecessary, but this is counterproductive to creativity. You can't be creative if you're not seeing the whole picture. Anyone prone to dismissing information or categorizing selective inputs as irrelevant is less creative. Creative people want more stimuli and to process as much as they can, or they won't be able to create new ideas. They work on increasing their knowledge, intelligence, and the white matter that sends pulses from one neuron to the next.

Your conscious mind is constantly consuming stimulation, and the only way to prevent creative genius from turning into mental dysfunction is to slowly and gradually increase your knowledge and decrease your latent inhibition. That's why we can't change habits overnight either. Learn new habits slowly, experiment with new ideas gradually, and allow the basal ganglia region of your brain to expand correctly. Even meditation gurus suggests that you practice slowly over time to master the art of controlling your selective input. Meditation isn't having latent inhibition. It's merely a gentle and slow skill that decreases your inhibitions and improves your ability to process more information slowly.

Practicing your talents and creativity can also allow the white matter in your brain to form and strengthen new connections gradually. Creativity might've been born overnight when your mother gave birth to you, but it's a slow journey back. Once mastered, you'll be like the musicians that get lost in their music. They don't block environmental stimuli out just for the sake of finding it irrelevant. They learn to be selective on their own terms. You must ensure that any new pathways or habits in the brain are creative too. Don't absorb information that counteracts ingenuity.

Think of your brain as an incredibly intricate garden with multiple bonsai trees. The inputs must be regulated consciously so that your bonsai trees don't die. Bonsai trees require perfect balance and masterful intent, as they're one of the most sensitive trees on earth. Tending to your garden and nurturing those trees that will ensure that you find the precise creative genius you need to flourish.

Optimizing Your Bonsai Connections

Being selective means that everything you do from today on must be conducive to your garden, and practice will only make your bonsais grow into strong trees. It's not just what you put into your brain, but it's also about the lifestyle you lead.

Exercise is one method of transforming your garden into something incredible. Have you noticed how happy and positive exercise enthusiasts appear? Workouts aren't only good for keeping you in shape. It feeds the brain like you'd give nutrients to your garden. It can expand your creativity and enhance memory storage. Considering that your imagination and ideas come from memories, now you understand why it improves your creativity.

Memory consolidation is enhanced when exercise helps release chemicals that strengthen the pulse connections to enhance habits further (Loria, 2016). Brain-derived neurotrophic factor (BDNF) is released during exercise and it encourages neurological growth or the increase in white matter. Aerobic exercises are a great start, so go for a walk, jog, or swim.

Dehydration is another common problem when you lack ingenuity. Unfortunately, the body and mind respond to it by releasing hormones that don't strengthen your pulse connections. The brain can function better when it's receiving enough nutritional support, and water is just one of the many products it needs. Your memory and concentration are improved and this kicks your creativity awake. The more efficient the brain becomes, the more masterful you are of your creativity.

The brain and gut have a connection like no other, as the stomach and its contents can affect the brain. Incorrect diets have led to mental health disruptions, and any attack on the brain is an attack on your ingenuity. Doctor Fernando Gómez-Pinilla from UCLA analyzed 160 studies confirming the influence of the stomach on your thinker (Alnuweiri, 2018). Gómez-Pinilla believes that food acts as a pharmacological drug inside the stomach to offset your hormones and brain chemistry if you're not eating right. It's a scary thought but you can eat better to sustain creative genius.

Fruit and vegetables have proven to boost creativity, and whole grains, seaweed, bananas, and almonds are hailed as brain food. You don't have to diet to be creative, you only have to eat natural foods. Excess sugar can cause your brain to deteriorate and natural foods containing flavonoids and tyrosine boost creativity, enhance your focus, and aid memory consolidation. Your critical-thinking mind is also boosted. Many people don't connect the critical mind to the creative side, but creativity is problem-solving after all. Dark chocolate also sparks inspiration, so you aren't staying away from everything tasty. You're simply keeping it natural and consuming fewer preservatives, additives, refined sugar, and processed foods.

Sleep, or lack of, is the final piece of the puzzle that could make you the new Mozart or it can deplete whatever creativity exists. Sleep improves your concentration, critical-thinking, attention, responses, decisions, and creativity (John, 2019). It also enhances your memory consolidation, learning ability, coordination, social skills, and overall well-being. Our brains cycle through five stages of sleep every 90 minutes. The first four stages are called non-rapid-eye movement sleep (non-REM), and the final stage is called rapid-eye-movement sleep (REM). The first four stages are where your body restores itself physically, but it's the REM stage that matters for creativity.

Brain cells shrink to allow faster pulses between neurons and the toxic beta-amyloid protein is removed while sleeping. The speed at which your brain works in the REM stage is the reason all your memories are stored long-term and you're capable of learning from them. You need to learn from memories to create something new. Sleep disruptions slow down your brain function during this crucial stage, and you could be left feeling incomprehensible. That's why sleep-deprived people have to ask someone to repeat themselves before they understand them. The brain can't generate new ideas when it's tired.

Take care of your brain, and give it the attention and respect it deserves and it will return the favor with a plethora of masterful creativity. Now, you know how to nurture the heart and brain so that you can use them together. Keep tending to your bonsai trees and feed them only what they flourish with.

Chapter 3:

Embodying Your Role as a Creative Genius

Creativity might exist in your biology and evolution, but it isn't something that simply lingers about and waits for you to master it. Ingenuity is cultivated and exercised until it becomes second nature. Becoming your true self and feeding your mind with the knowledge about brains and hearts is only the start. It's time to use the information you've learned so far and apply creative genius in everything you do from this point onwards. Use this chapter to learn how to move from the good to the elite, and finally, to the unstoppable creative.

20 Golden Rules of Unstoppable Creativity

Unstoppable creatives are in a league of their own. Being one means that you won't be competing with anyone but yourself. You won't give people the chance to think, doubt, and question your artwork, but people will feel a deep urge to respond to it. The first actionable step to becoming a creative genius is to claim the title. Stop talking about your ingenuity as something you're busy improving, a skill you're learning, or a goal you want to pursue. Embody your title and everything that comes with it. Talk to yourself and other people as though your creativity already exists. Don't say that you're going to pursue your writing or music. Rather say: "I am a writer, or I am the new musical prodigy."

Has anyone ever told you to dress for the job you want? That's because embodying yourself presently in the title is powerful enough to trick the brain into believing it. Turn your passion for art into reality and step up to the unstoppable plate. Apply everything you learned at the end of Chapter Two, including improved sleep and eating brain food. Don't forget to stand in your truth as you learned in Chapter One. Finally, own your title by following the 20 unstoppable rules of creative genius. Owning your title also allows you to own your behavior, responses, and choices.

Rule One: Be Prepared for Everything

Practice your creativity so that you can master it while everyone else is relaxing. Learn the rules of society, the laws that regulate artistry, and then, throw them all away. Redesign what people think is real and bring new life to old ideas. Expanding your intelligence will also enhance your consciousness gradually and time will move slower for you. You'll have more time to see various perspectives and question each one. Even when inspiration hits, practice and allow trial and error to guide you to perfection. Expecting more, learning more, and knowing that people are malleable, evolutionary creatures will help you stay prepared.

Rule Two: Forget About Materialism

Materialism provides false security and happiness. Remove it and you'll feel determined to reach higher. Never allow materialistic things like money to direct your creativity. Yes, you'd love to be wealthy, but money has never made anyone happy. Your reward must be to create the best and nothing else.

Rule Three: Always Seek More

The previous rule snowballs into this one. True creative geniuses are never satisfied with what they have because being ingenious means that you always challenge what exists. There's always a way to make it better, more beautiful, more soulful, and even more valuable. Don't set your eyes on menial goals, but rather focus on the journey. Not looking for inspiration while your eyes are locked onto a single target is like the wolf becoming blind. Unstoppable people are humble and grateful for every achievement, but they know the best way to be their greatest selves is to set new goals every time they accomplish the last one.

Rule Four: Use Masterful Self-Control

The only person in control of what you create is you. Manage your time and control all the factors that contribute to your brain and heart health. Make sure that you're allocating enough time to pursue the right inspiration and that there's plenty left for working on your projects. Set time aside for writing daily if you're an author. Don't allow your creations or time to control you; you must control them.

Rule Five: Don't Loosen the Reins

This might sound stressful but never let go of the pressure you feel to be the best singer, musician, writer, sculptor, or painter. A healthy amount of pressure is necessary to keep you from becoming complacent. Complacency leads to laziness and lost inspiration. Keep pushing yourself while maintaining self-care and self-compassion. Find your balance because letting down your guard will unravel every bit of momentum you have.

Rule Six: Challenge People

Indeed, unstoppable creatives never compete with anyone but themselves; however, you want to challenge people to compete with you. You fail to be your true self if you keep slowing down and checking to see how others are progressing. Take inspiration, but be careful not to subconsciously mimic other people by keeping checks on them. Zone back into your truth and remain authentic. Once unstoppable, other people will feel the need to compete with you.

Rule Seven: Don't Stop Your Intelligence Expansion

Extraordinary and unstoppable creatives seek knowledge and inspiration above entertainment. Focus on learning more and your mind will thank you by giving you new ideas. Anyone who throws their hands in the air and says "enough, I know more than I need to," is the person who trips over their own feet. Masters and creative geniuses know that there's no such thing as knowing enough.

Rule Eight: Take Responsibility

Just as you own your title, you must own your mistakes. Be proud of the work you've created that isn't as valuable as the last one. Not every piece of art will carry the same value. Don't blame yourself or wallow in guilt if you've created something offensive either. Check your ego and remember to possess humility in perfect balance with confidence. Admitting to mistakes and failures is how we learn from them. Be honest with yourself about what happened and develop a plan to move forward.

Rule Nine: Allow Creativity to Express Itself

What's more expressive than actions or a showcase of absolute creativity? Allow your art to speak for itself because it contains your essence, soul, and ingenuity.

Art should be deep and not shallow. Deep creativeness is rare, non-replicable, and carries high value. Shallow art contains commonality, no value, and is easily copied. Remember that you're challenging other artists to be better than you. You'll never allow it if you keep your creative edge alive, but it's a necessity to make others want to compete with you. Even writers must abide by this rule because talk is cheap. Therefore, words are cheap unless they're deep.

Rule Ten: Exercise Your Greatest Muscle

Why focus your learning only on your chosen artistic field? You need to mentally exercise the brain because it's also a muscle. Extend your knowledge into matters that aren't creative because you might see something that no one else thought was phenomenal until you recreated it. Stop looking at what everyone else is creating and live a life beyond your medium. Go on adventures and participate in every activity you can. Seek inspiration far enough and it will come to you before you know it.

Rule Eleven: Remain Confident

Confidence will determine what goals you make, whether you reach them, and how quickly you bounce back from failures. Don't stop working on your confidence or you'll become a sheep again. Striving to become the top illustrator in your country is not only a physical marathon. It's a mental journey, and you'll need to fuel it with confidence to persevere. Being confident is not being afraid to try new things, and art is a constant flow of new ideas after all.

Rule Twelve: Let Go

This is a two-part rule. Let go of anything that holds you back emotionally. Don't envy others or feel disappointed because they created something better. Instead, forgive the baggage you carry, but the second part of the rule means that you must never forget it. Forgive yourself for coming in second, but allow yourself to grow from the experience. Emotional baggage and the inability (or unwillingness) to forgive are heavy burdens to lug around.

Rule Thirteen: Forget Hesitation

Hesitation is the father of lost opportunities. The truth is that the anticipation of displaying your artwork at the gallery is more frightening than the event itself. Fear is what drives hesitation. Train yourself to forget that hesitation exists and to respond to inspiration immediately. Do you know how many times a writer has a brilliant idea, and they think they're capable of remembering it the next day? Ideas are lost, inspiration vanishes, but writing down your ideas or immediately implementing them is a great way to ensure that you never lose them.

Rule Fourteen: Simplicity is the Key

Many artists expand their minds to surpass the evolutionary trajectory of their work. They connect dots that other people aren't capable of connecting yet. Not everyone is intelligent, unfortunately, and I don't mean this as an insult to anyone. Simplicity and sophistication are connected like conjoined twins. Creating something that everyone can understand is what makes your art valuable to them. You don't want every observer to ask you what it is. You don't want comments about how your art makes no sense. People must say: "Holy cow, now I get it!" Help people to reach enlightenment creatively.

Rule Fifteen: Share Accomplishments

The secret to being humble is when someone can share the extravagance of a colleague or another artist. Unstoppable creatives challenge other people for humble reasons, and that's why you should want what's best for them too. Their success isn't yours, but neither are their failures. Congratulate fellow artists on their work and question them deeply about what inspired them. Show an interest and allow them to inspire you. Feel proud of anyone who can separate themselves from the herd and display their honest passions.

Rule Sixteen: Shoot for Every Target

You *will* shoot and miss, and that's why you shouldn't allow opportunities or inspiration to slip past your radar. You're guaranteed to miss targets if you don't aim for any. Remember rule number 13, hesitation is the death of inspiration. Don't fear mistakes or failures. Everyone makes them, and it doesn't make you special. Being unstoppable, persistent, and eager to create more is what makes you special. It's also fine to start on something even before you're sure of it. Do you have any idea how many books I've written, rewritten, and edited months later again? Starting something is always a challenge but it's easier to act now and perfect it later.

Rule Seventeen: Commit to the 10-Fold Rule

Compounding interest is a great way to understand the 10-Fold rule. If you had to be 10 times better, faster, and less hesitant than any other artist, every time you create anything, including thoughts, you'd be 10 times better. Allow 10 thoughts for every inspiration you find. Look at 10 different options, and create 10 versions of it in your mind. Don't do what every sheep does. They think things through once and action it once. Commit to thinking, creating, and supplying 10 times the number of creative outputs, mentally or physically.

Photographers don't take one picture. They take multiple shots and choose the best one. Let's say that John photographed the fluffy albino tarantula, and he loves manual photo manipulation. He doesn't like digital cameras and prefers to set the exposure and light manually. Unfortunately, this tarantula that looks like a cuddly toy is rare. John forgets the 10-fold rule and loses his work because he snapped a few single pictures from various angles. He didn't take repeated shots to ensure that perfect photo.

Give yourself endless options when you paint, write, sketch, or play an instrument. If you put in 10 times the effort, you'll earn 10 times the rewards.

Rule Eighteen: Make Downtime a Priority

You're always chasing the next goal, but self-care requires you to apply downtime. Overworking yourself won't help you achieve your goals, but that's why you're focused on the journey and not just the results. Everyone needs time to rest and recover, even unstoppable creatives. The way you can distinguish downtime from hesitation and procrastination is that you'll be planning it. Rule number one told you to be prepared for everything, and that includes downtime.

Creating art and inspiring others at the level of unstoppable creatives requires a lot of strength and stamina. They know when to take a break and pause the marathon. Just make sure your planned rest is rejuvenating, though. Don't spend a night on the town when you have a great idea to paint tomorrow. Rather spend time with friends, journal, listen to music, meditate, or do anything you love that isn't directly associated with your medium. Hobbies don't include things you're making money from in this sense.

Rule Nineteen: Act Without Permission

This sounds like another broken societal law, but it's more complicated than that. If you need to ask anyone's permission to start your artistic endeavors, then you probably shouldn't do it. First, you wouldn't be asking loved ones if they approve if you were being true to yourself. Secondly, only you know what you desire. Your family and friends can be supportive, or sadly, they can try to convince you that you're making a mistake because creatives make no money.

However, you decide what direction your life takes. You're not living by their rules anymore and in that sense, yes, you're breaking your inner community's rules. You don't need approval or permission to be great. Otherwise, you're not being authentic or trusting yourself. You'll be who you choose to be, and creative ever finds happiness in following the family business.

Rule Twenty: Don't Break Commitments

I feel like this final rule sums the rest of them up. Indeed, every decision you make, every stride you take towards goals, and every commitment you make is a promise made to yourself. Breaking this promise will leave you with emotional baggage you can't carry. Stick to your plan and get up when you need to. Who knows what you'll miss if you sleep late on a morning you were supposed to attend a lecture at the gallery? That lecture could've changed your life forever. Allowing any of your boundaries, rules, commitments, or promises to falter will only make you stoppable. You know what you want, so go and get it.

These are the rules no creative can live without. Follow the rules of creative geniuses and be the unstoppable force in the art world, whatever your medium might be.

Supplementing the Rules

Always follow the unstoppable rules, but some of them contain supporting information that could supplement their implementation. Certain characteristics, skills, tenaciousness, and goal pursuits are required to traverse the rules without fail.

Honoring Desire

Desire is the force that drives who we were, are now, and who we'll become. It's the passion inside of us that feeds off the rewards we achieve. The primal survival instinct is a desire, but so is the need to create art. Desire and rewards are like oxygen that keeps the embers of your life burning. Without it, life becomes dull and boring. A friend of mine spent years being unhappy. She always dreamed of being an actress, but her family convinced her to stop wasting her time. Her friends told her she was too shy. Her drama teacher called her adrift in the waters of dying theater.

I'm sure you're starting to understand why I don't respect teachers too much. Many of them are great, but they're unsuspecting role models to kids and can certainly take a child's spark away. Anyway, Sarah never chose to try because she wasn't true to her desires. She didn't honor her desires, and that's why the best years of her life were menial at best. It wasn't until she reached her late thirties that she decided to honor her desires. She took some classes and sent her headshot to agents. Sarah was a gorgeous woman but in an unusual way. She had a certain attitude that permeated through static photos.

It wasn't long before agents lined up at her door, and guess what? The producer called her a phenomenal expression of everything the world needs. You see, Sarah didn't honor her desires for years and maybe she would've failed at first. However, she was shocked to realize that her desires gave wind to the embers that ignited self-actualization. Always honor your desires, but the only secret is that you must listen to them first. Listening before acting will help you devise a concise plan to reach the rewards you deserve. Unstoppable creatives always gather knowledge and inspiration first.

It helps them design goals that ignite the embers needed to carry you to an old-age where you know that life was worth living. Desires often manifest themselves as instincts or gut-feelings too. Honoring your desires also gives your life structure and meaning. It leads you to a certain future instead of having insecurities about creative urges.

Keep Growing

Unstoppable creatives never stop learning. Self-growth can never stop gaining momentum and there are endless reasons why you'd want to gather every ounce of information your brain can hold before it implodes psychologically. Don't worry, you won't lose your mind, as long as you're practicing self-care and gradually growing on a slow journey.

Learning more and improving yourself fertilizes happiness because you're constantly reaching higher and earning more. Everything comes second to the rewards when you experience them. Think about how you'll feel the first time you created a painting of value when you've allowed learned knowledge to piece it together.

Knowledge also makes you more valuable to your support team and other artists. You're more adaptable and can help others find creative solutions to their problems. For example, people appreciate someone they can have a meaningful conversation with. It doesn't help if you only photograph incredible images. What inspired you? How did your mind piece the puzzle together?

Willing and curious people are also humble. They don't act like an arrogant know-it-all, and are prepared to listen to other viewpoints. Being humble means that you can accept input from other people without it interrupting your artistic flow. People are also more likely to be inspired by a humble person who welcomes them to grow in their knowledge together. Leaders and mentors are knowledgeable people who aren't afraid of learning more and sharing their insights. Therefore, you might inspire other people when you're always humbly curious.

You'll also become more interesting, attractive, and deeper, making your social life burst with energy. Imagine being able to help a friend because you happened to learn about vegetation in your pursuit to find inspiration. She's having an issue with garden pests and you learned that certain flowers attract them while researching your next creation. Your respect will also grow towards other people because we require understanding to show true empathy. You can't understand how frustrated your friend is about learning a new cord on the violin if you know nothing about the process.

However, some research can help you connect deeper to this person by understanding that the violin is the hardest instrument to play. Most new musicians think it can be strung like a guitar. They don't realize that it requires perfect gentleness and patience. Always needing to know more can also expose desires you haven't noticed before. These desires can turn into your masterpiece if you honor them instead of unknowingly ignoring them. Making new friends, being more helpful, and increasing your overall value are some of the benefits of learning more.

To top this, you'll also know that you're growing every time you learn something that helps you create more new ideas. Finally, the brain remains a muscle and unless you exercise it, it will age and wither (Kayte, 2020). Yes, you can slow down the aging process and potential degeneration by training your brain daily.

Being Humble

Humility is required to be unstoppable, inside and out. Humble people have shown to handle stress better and improve their overall health (Allan, 2014). It's a soul-soothing characteristic to develop because it helps us look behind the face of tragedy and this is how we overcome stress. We don't see death as the end, but rather another perspective. This offers us an alternative to the depression and anxiety that comes with stress. Stress alone can impact the heart, brain, and every system in your body.

Humility teaches you to prioritize meaningful things that improve your life. Your relationships flourish, and you possess gratitude and generosity that doesn't make you negotiate your boundaries. Gratitude isn't some substrate, how can we know we've arrived at one destination if we won't accept the reward? Humility also offers freedom from the fears of hiding who you are and what you desire. Self-control is another benefit of being humble. You can prioritize yourself and be generous, kind, and grateful at the same time.

It teaches discipline and appreciation for the little things. Besides, kindness towards other people releases dopamine and endorphins in the brain and these are natural happiness chemicals. Being kind to others can make you happier as long as you remain steadfast in your boundaries. Humility is learned. It won't happen overnight, but it will develop as your creativity does.

Help people in need when you can because this extends the kindness that tricks your brain into fulfillment. It also exercises generosity and helps you grow your gratitude further because you'll appreciate the life you have when you volunteer at the homeless shelter or donate unwanted clothes. Heck, donate some art supplies to help someone else reach their dreams.

Practice self-compassion and mindfulness to assert humility. You'll learn to know yourself better and will stick to the boundaries that prioritize you without being arrogant about it. Mindfulness and meditation make you aware of thoughts and emotions without being judgmental or condescending towards yourself.

Don't forget to exercise your gratitude either. Thank someone for doing the most menial thing today and try to thank another person tomorrow. Commit yourself to show gratitude daily and reward yourself for the progress you've made because it's thanks to the hard-working person inside of you.

Finally, you should never be scared to ask for help. Humble people won't fear the judgment of other people when they've messed up. Remember that you're responsible for your mistakes too and this is part of being humble.

The Art of Planning

Goals are the foundation of most of the rules to be creatively unstoppable. Sadly, many people fail because they don't know how to set goals correctly for guaranteed achievements. Goals are about more than just surviving, you'll fail without deeper meaning and attaching your desires to them. Daily routines set our objectives, but life goals are what we wish to achieve over a period. They direct you and make you accountable for reaching your dreams. You know what you desire and what your life should look like to make you happy, but clear goals can mean so much more.

It will clarify the behaviors you need for when, how, and where you'll implement the actions to get to the outcome. Clarity can make things a lot simpler.

Clear goals also give you the option of getting feedback which can help you learn more.

It promotes happiness every time you reach a milestone because you know what they look like. This increases your motivation to continue your journey.

Clear goals can also help you harness the power of your greatest strengths, you know what's needed to get what you want. You have to be true to yourself to be creative. You also need to be humble to be unstoppable.

Goals offer us two kinds of rewards. You have intrinsic and extrinsic pursuits. The former will develop emotional gratitude, self-growth, purpose, and intimacy. The latter kind promotes success, status, and wealth. Intrinsic goals are intimately conformed to further your desires, whereas extrinsic goals impact the lives of other people or are related to universal factors, such as wealth. Intrinsic goals also promote self-actualization and happiness. Internally motivated goals would include using your creativity to develop a new idea into something previously unfathomable.

It also includes the goals you set for promoting mental health, knowledge, and self-promotion. Moreover, they focus on your relationships and help in developing humility. Externally motivated goals aren't frowned upon because you can commit to owning your own studio in five years or earning enough money from your art to buy the home of your dreams. However, for self-growth, you'll focus mainly on intrinsic goals. Prioritize your goals before you create an actionable plan. Start by choosing five goals, both long and short-term.

Don't focus too much on the details yet. Just jot them down and give them each a score between one and 10. One means that you're unsure if you want the exact outcome, whereas 10 would be the goals you refuse to negotiate with. Your most important goals are intrinsic, and they follow your desires. Now, design an actionable plan because the reason people fail is that they don't set step-by-step plans.

Actionable Goals

Learn a new word because it's going to be a good friend of yours. The word SMART translates to specific, measurable, attainable, relevant, and timely. Design a colorful display and stick it somewhere that reminds you to be SMART.

The goals you've chosen are the outcomes of each desire. It's the end result and gives you a destination you can work back from. Every goal must be SMART. Is it specific, like releasing the new solo you've been working on? Define the solo and be clear about any details of your goal. You must be able to envision every aspect of it. What shirt are you wearing? Where are you standing? Who is with you and how do you feel in the moment that you share your creation?

The M asks whether the goal is measurable? Yes it is, because you can write one verse daily for the next two weeks. So, the action steps for this goal is to spend an hour every day for 14 days with your pen and paper. Once again, you must be able to envision the steps you take to reach the goal. Let's say that you have a longer goal. You want to paint Cat Island, which is a Japanese island full of domestic-type cats that chill on the beach as though they own the place. Well, they do own the place. Anyway, your measurable milestones must be actionable.

You'd have to visit Japan and take the Ferry to see and experience the island yourself. This is broken into further steps where you apply for your passport. Every tiny step must also be specific. So, you'd even have to imagine standing in the awful queue to get your passport. Use your senses to fully engage in the vision. Keep breaking every actionable step into smaller fragments until you have a step-by-step plan. Every step must have a timeframe as well. For example, you'll apply for your passport by Tuesday.

Is your goal achievable? Well, you're a songwriter and you have the talent to create. So, for the short-term songwriter's goal, it's achievable. For the painter, it might seem more daunting. That's why we break it down into smaller actions, because setting a goal to travel to a foreign island just to paint ginger cats on the beach seems extravagant, but looking at the little actions instead of the entire picture can help you determine whether it's achievable. Don't accidentally set yourself up for failure. It's hard to achieve a dream of heading to Japan if you can barely afford an air ticket to Florida.

Is the goal relevant to you? Yes, to both examples. The songwriter's passion is creating unique songs and sharing them. The painter's dream is also realistic because he desires to paint the unusual. Most people have never heard of Cat Island. He doesn't only want to paint it, but he also wants to experience it to gather greater inspiration. Who knows, he might see something else while he's there. The relevant part simply reminds you to make sure your goals are truly desirable.

The time consuming part is where you choose exact dates and when you want this goal to be achieved. This includes all the mini-goals that you complete before reaching the main one.

Now, it's time to pursue your goals. Don't worry about motivation, as this comes naturally thanks to your reticular activating system (RAS). This part of your brain is tricked when you keep envisioning your goals with every sense you can implement. The rule of RAS says that what you see is what you achieve (Ho, 2006). Motivation isn't only needed for starting your goals, it also gains momentum when you reach milestones and get closer to the outcome. The final part of creating and following a masterful action plan is to keep track of your progress and reward achievements.

Rewards always lead to more motivation, but you won't see the progress unless you're paying attention to the milestone achievements. Tracking could also help you see new avenues or ideas along the way. Return daily to your short-term goals to visualize your outcome and check off any minor achievements along the way. Do the same with long-term goals but give them appropriate visualization return times. Don't be disheartened when you miss a step either. Get up and move forward again because it happens to the best of us. Avoid missing steps by setting reminders on your phone.

Trust Yourself: Toss Plan B

Creative geniuses never give up, no matter what! There's no such thing as plan B in unstoppable creatives. You'll only be limiting your true potential when you give yourself an escape route. There's nothing more motivating than having no backup plan. Compare your action plan to marriage. Do spouses have backup plans or does this imply a lack of faith, loyalty, trust, commitment, and sincerity? That's my point. There's nothing wrong with having people keep tabs on you and hold you accountable.

In fact, having friends hold you accountable to your action plan A is recommended, but don't have them hold on to a separate plan for when you stumble on the first one. Scientists at Wharton and Wisconsin researched the effects of having a contingency plan to see if participants would accomplish their goals if they knew there was another way (Dooley, 2016). Participants had to complete tasks under two conditions. The first group was simply asked to complete the task while the second group had to think about what would happen if they failed.

The results proved that motivation and commitment die with a backup plan. The plan B group was significantly less successful in completing the task. You could botch your goals if you allow the chance of redirection. Unstoppable creatives commit every ounce of energy to their goals and achieve them as long as their desires were catered to.

Becoming the next creative genius that everyone talks about, even those who doubted you, is just 20 rules away. Use the supplementary evidence to understand how each rule guarantees success. Be curious, set goals, and reach for beyond the stars by dedicating yourself to the embodiment of creativity.

Chapter 4:

The Power of Feng Shui

Now that you have the internal embodiment of creative genius, you can set your eyes on the external part. A change of scenery is more powerful than you think. The environment impacts your flow, and it either conducts you or you can direct it like the wolf you're becoming. The world, in all its glory, can either make you creative or stifle your attempts. Using Feng Shui will allow you to influence the environment to make sure it's conducive to your flow. It's an ancient art that's inspired science, and applying it makes you even more unstoppable.

The Feng Shui Story

Feng Shui translates directly to wind and water from ancient Chinese scriptures. It's the flow we have with the world around us just as wind glides through the mountains and water flows through the rivers. You might be unique in every aspect, but one truth cannot be denied. You're part of the world, including the air, earth, and water. We call this nature, and what are humans other than part of nature? You're created in utter beauty just as the most powerful waterfall. You're just as complicated as the deepest depths of the ocean. You are nature and that's why you ground yourself back into the earth whenever you need stability.

Feng Shui is the art of controlling the flow of the environment to make it conducive to our passions, desires, and creativity. Feng Shui has been applied in the modern world to create environments conducive to happiness and fulfillment, in the home and workspaces. Entire constructs have been erected with geomantic designs intended to promote better workflows and home lives. Your body is connected deeply to the 'qui' or natural energy that flows through everything in nature. Conducting the flow is as simple as changing the environment so that your energy flows in harmony.

Colors, shapes, elements, layouts, and framework are all factors that have their own energies. We call it energy and scientists refer to it as perpetuating particles that make up everything that exists. Feng Shui was so protected and secretive that few scriptures escaped China since it was first used more than 6,000 years ago (Emmer, 2018). Most people know the story of the ancient Chinese farming villages that were auspiciously placed between mountain ranges to ensure that the strong winds didn't ruin them, while the rivers ran through them to sustain life. The least prosperous villages were outside of the Feng Shui placements and were torn by winds and arid without water.

Many powerful leaders and military men hailed from the prosperous villages and that's why Feng Shui was one of the most highly guarded secrets in Imperial China. The secrets were forbidden from anyone but the heirs to the military figures. Fu Xi was one of the first emperors in China between 2952 and 2836 BC, and he was famed for holding the secrets. He founded the eight trigrams depicted in the Bagua or placement map. He understood long before Westernized science that energy is forever perpetual, but he perceived the eight principles which distinguish it from the western understanding. The different principle energies collide with and alter each other, much like quantum physics teaches us.

These principles stood for the earth, thunder, sky, mountain, water, fire, marsh, and wind, and they represented the principle energies that correlated to the placement of villages. The Bagua's eight segments represent colors, shapes, elements, numbers, and anything made of energy. Following the Bagua allows us to flow with the energy of nature. Xi also received two spiritual gifts from the Yellow River when a "dragon-horse" walked out of the river with black and white numerical dots on its back. This is where the idea of yin and yang first stirred because the dragon-horse represented a perfectly balanced life.

The same pattern was observed on a tortoise shell after the tortoise escaped from the Luo River during a great flood. This time, the numerical dots were placed carefully into eight fragments that surrounded a square. There was an emphasis on the center block which led

Xi to believe that the person controlling the Feng Shui is the ninth principle. However, the tortoise, also called the *Luo Shu*, represents a deeper lesson than the dragon-horse. It showed a consistent pattern when the numerals were observed. The three by three grid aligned to the number 15 every time it was calculated diagonally, or by row or column. The Chinese have a 15-year cycle in their calendar and that's how Xi knew that the energy was ever-changing.

This brought about the book of changes, which is one of the oldest Chinese texts. The book was completed roughly around the Zhou Dynasty between 1022 and 256 BC. The eight groups of solid and broken lines that represent yin and yang found in the Bagua map were further divided into 64 principles. Confucius revered the book and taught its philosophy as understanding the constant perpetual energy in the universe. Simply, Confucians taught that everything you send into the world, returns. Yin and yang suggest that opposite energies complement each other best. This is understood as day and night, dark or light, and death and life. Feng Shui balances the yin and yang energy exchange between you and the environment.

More realizations came from the study of these principles. *Wu Xing* was developed which represents the five elements of wood, fire, water, metal, and earth. Ancient philosophers and modern-day physicists understand that every particle of energy needs to interact with another one. Wood is changed by fire and fire is doused by the earth. Earth forms metal, metal is impenetrable by water, and water gives life to wood.

However, each element can overcome another one. Wood overcomes earth, fire makes metal malleable, Earth controls water, metal confines wood, and water douses fire as well. It shows cyclic perpetual motion between elements.

Finally, the Chinese compass was developed. The ancients needed to understand how magnetic forces can also alter energy flows. Physicists know that gravitational particles called photons are different from regular energies because of the magnetic component. Ancient Chinese believed that every magnetic force is either positive or negative, such as yin and yang, or north and south. The Chinese used the eight principles, correlating elements that represented various energies, and the direction of the sun and the north star, to design the compass that helps us understand how the heavens and earth are all encumbered into one electromagnetic field.

The first Chinese compass needle is as old as 4,000 BC, but it wasn't until the Warring States Period between 475 and 221 BC that it was connected to Feng Shui. Now, Feng Shui has become the most valuable practice in China. The practitioners used the directional magnetism of elements and aligned them with environmental changes to create perfect buildings and villages.

Environmental Influence

The Chinese were smart people and their advancements were similar to what we see in physics today. Other than the tactical and survival advantages of Bagua mapping, it all comes back to where it started. The villages between the mountains knew that building their farmsteads in the right positions would allow them to prosper. They took the natural energy around them and used it to their advantage. Fast-forward to today, and look at what science says about the environment's influence on you. The environment includes the people you surround yourself with, the media you consume, the books you read, and even the Netflix series you watch. Your environment is so influential because it includes everything that can stimulate your senses. Most importantly, it's everything physically surrounding you! The environment controls how creative you do or do not feel, and how and when creative energy comes or doesn't come to you. It can make you hit a creative brick wall or it can make you bulldoze right through it. Your senses are picking up constant changes in the environment as you move from place to place, and the stimulus forms thoughts and emotions. How many times have you walked into a room darkened by deep blue shades and felt eerily sad? Yes, dark blue is the color of knowledge, but overwhelming amounts of it can offset your energy and make you question yourself.

It's negative yang energy, if overused and not balanced by a yin counterpart. It comes back to science now because your particles vibrate with certain energy frequencies (Bardsley, 2018). Colors also vibrate energy frequencies and the dark blue might not be vibrating at the same frequency as you. Your energy collision with that of the overpowering color can cause a positive charge in your particles. The human body can only withstand so much positive charge before it overloads. This leads to mood disorders and hormonal changes in the body. Being in an environment that doesn't vibrate the right frequencies does the same. Opposites will attract as yin and yang do, and the energies will start colliding.

Mental health will decline if the environment isn't balanced. Roger Ulrich from Texas University and Craig Zimring from the Georgia Institute of Technology wanted to test the Feng Shui theory (Ulrich et al., 2004). Patients aren't happy in hospitals and that's no secret, but Ulrich and Zimring chose to compare patients with a view of some vibrational Feng Shui to those who had a view of a brick wall. Not surprisingly, the patients with a better view healed faster and were discharged before their no-view counterparts. The environment, especially the physical part of it, can help patients recover by making them feel less stressed and safer.

Patients who recover in empty and lonely rooms without any environmental stimulants also take longer to recover. Bustling spaces, and creating the physical environment around you is the way you keep your mood from faltering. You don't want harmful hormones released. You also don't want to feel stressed. Stress leads to many complications, such as heart disease, blood pressure issues, and stroke. These conditions hurt your brain or heart that are the soul and thinker behind the creative genius. Even rooms with more light can create better energy flows and that explains another reason why the person became overwhelmed in the darkened room. Dark rooms must be saved for bedtime.

Depression, agitation, and sleep disorders have less chance of affecting you in a well-lit and controlled space. The environment will even discourage social interactions if it's not vibrating with balanced energy. You don't want people to avoid you just because your creative workspace is in the basement. The benefits of a Feng Shui creation station in your home are phenomenal, but it also extends to every environment you're in frequently. For example, it doesn't help to have a workspace where you flow with nature, and then you sleep in a bedroom that causes upset. Manipulate every home and work environment, from a hobby room to the family room.

Creating conducive environments throughout the home is great if you're working from home too because it allows you to divide your creative space from the sleep, social, and overall home-life to create normalcy. Most artists work from home, and their home/work balance is tainted by the pressure of having to be creative during designated family and leisure time. Anyone who works from home also knows that we take fewer breaks because where could we escape for lunch if our kitchen is within eyesight from our canvases? The creative benefits of having your flow space should also be considered.

You'll have fewer distractions, and your mind can really focus on what matters. Besides, you'll also save loads of money if you set up shop at home. This only applies to people renting a studio or sitting at coffee shops because they find their homes too loud and distracting for writing. No doubt, there are many reasons to become a Feng Shui master of your creation station now. Focus all your Feng Shui powers onto the home space where you work and extend them into the rooms that offer support and balance.

The Basics of Bagua Mapping

The intentional manipulation of the physical environment, particularly the materialistic side of it, is what you're going to do. It's best to have a basic understanding of the Bagua map first though.

You need to position yourself as the ninth principle in the room. There's a command position to learn when you use Feng Shui. Every room is divided into a three by three diagram of equal squares when you walk into the door. The command position is the center point of your vision when you walk into the room if you divide the floor into nine squares. Ancient Chinese used this position in military tactics to dominate the center of the strategy. Yes, they even used Feng Shui in military formations. The command position got its name because it was only military commanders who knew the secrets of Feng Shui.

It also makes more sense being diagonally placed so that your sight is always towards the door. We unknowingly prefer sitting with our backs to the wall so that no one can surprise us from the doorway. Walk into any office and see how the desks are placed. Backs are to the windows so that the worker can pay attention to the priority, which is whatever or whoever comes through the door. Expect anything and always be prepared, right? It's a rule of unstoppable creatives too. The command position puts you in control of the room.

The eight principles in the three-by-three diagram you face as you walk into the room correlate to various colors, shapes, seasons, and elements. Even body parts are connected to each space.

The wealth principle is the top-left corner and it represents prosperity, fortune, and abundance. It resonates with purple and rectangular shapes. It's a springtime wooden element that flows with yin. It also relates to the wind and protects your hips.

The fame principle is the top-center space and it represents reputation, visibility, and passion. It's shown as red triangles or pointy shapes. It's a summertime fire element that's connected to your eyes.

The top-right corner is the partnership principle that represents relationships, love for yourself and partners, marriage, and self-care. It's a pink square or flat shape. It's an earthly yin element that belongs in the transitional period of seasons. This principle connects to your heart, abdomen, and other organs below the neck.

The center-left space is the family and health principle that covers new beginnings. It's presented in green, blue, or teal rectangular shapes. It's a yang type wooden element that correlates best with spring. It's also complemented by thunder and connects to the feet.

The very center of the room is the self-principle that represents well-being, grounding, mind, body, and soul. Any shape that's flat or square, and is brown, orange, or yellow fits it. It's an earthly element that often works best during seasonal transitions. This is the space for everything you stand for.

The center-right space is the creative and children principle that represents joy, completion, desires, and fulfillment. It's circular or spherical with white or metallic coloring. It's a fall metal element that belongs to yin. It can also be complemented by water and represents the mouth.

The bottom-left corner is the wisdom principle that represents self-cultivation, knowledge, and skillfulness. It's a flat or square dark blue shape. It's an earth element that flows with yang and is best used in seasonal transitions. Your hands represent it best.

The bottom-center space is the career principle that represents pathways in life. It's normally a wave or curvy black shape. It's also a wintery water element that correlates to the ears.

The bottom-right corner is the helpful people principle that represents benefactors, purpose, and travel. It's circular or spherical and has gray or metallic colors. It's a fall-time metal element that belongs to yang, and it correlates to the head and brain.

Each of the five elements also contains certain energies that further complement or encourage the Bagua principles to enhance the effects of them.

Earth is grounded in self-care and stability and complements health, relationships, and knowledge.

Metal shows perfection, precision, efficiency, and beauty. It can also complement helpful people and children.

Water shows good flow, changes, and letting go. It complements your creative career.

Wood is an expansive element that's flexible, upward-moving, and offers vitality. It complements family and wealth principles.

Fire is passion, brilliance, and illumination, and it's always used to enhance the fame principle.

Now, you can see the room you walk into. Make notes of elements that could spark further creativity and the shapes, colors, and placements of them. Then, move onto redesigning each space in your home, depending on what you want in each block of every room. Start with your creation station first. Once you create one Feng Shui area, it will get easier to create more.

How to Feng Shui Your Home

Most people will want to target money, fame, or love, but unstoppable creatives will focus on more meaningful Feng Shui mapping. They'd look at the creativity and children principle and focus their attention on enhancing its energy. Children also don't mean procreation because they could represent rebirth, renewal, or the return to the inner child who's more creative than most adults. The creativity space can boost encouragement, generosity, and desires that align with your medium. It can help you empower your energy flows by improving all the factors required to enhance creativity.

Focus on this space if you desire more ingenuity, want to explore new ideas, have a creative block in your life, or want to regain child-like curiosity. The goals you set in Chapter Three could help you be specific about what your intentions are before mapping a room too. Intention is the beginning of a harmonious flow between you and the environment. Don't just say that you want to be more creative. Use the SMART system to set a goal before designing a certain space in your home. Setting your intention and knowing precisely what you desire is followed by clearing the area of all Feng Shui elements and principles that don't complement the space.

Take the wooden table out of the creative area and remove the mountain-view painting from the wall above it. Don't allow the wrong elements either. Take down the red curtains that interfere with the child-like creativity because it's fire and it belongs to fame. Red flames can also burn through your creative thoughts. Declutter the area because clutter represents wild and uncontrolled thoughts. You're cleaning the energy of the space. Do this throughout your home. Dirty windows also block the sunlight and prevents possibilities from entering your space. Be curious and welcome positive energy into a clean space.

Messy spaces are famous with artists, but clear the room before you start redesigning it. Don't be the stereotypical artist with paint all over their overalls with open cans and wet pallets lying around. Neat and tidy is where you start. Open the doors in your home too because you don't want to block the energy flowing through it. It will defeat the command position if you keep them shut. Remove clutter that blocks the door from opening at least 90 degrees. Express your creative desires in your wall-hangings by hanging them high and straight. Plan your colors according to your needs as well. Meaning, if you want a calm space, use lighter colors, and if you want a space that resonates with desired fame, then use bright reds.

The colors attached to each principle are merely guidelines. You can change the shades and use subtler, gentler, or bright colors. Your energy also vibrates better with colors that make you smile. Social spaces might do better with brighter colors again. Turn the family room into orange and brighter shades of green. Choose your color placements carefully according to their spaces too. Don't turn the whole room blood-red. The darkened blue room was Feng Shui's death and ignited enough wisdom energy to overpower you. You might also be stuck with some colors and shapes if you can't move items or furniture.

Try to decorate your home with moveable pieces because you'll be shifting your energy principles around often. Our desires evolve and so do our energy needs. So, don't go drilling holes in the wall for pictures unless you have loads of time to patch them up. Although, you can use nails if you have an assortment of artwork to change as your desires shift. A home without art on the wall doesn't belong to an artist. Using Feng Shui is a matter of thoughtfully planning the layout of your room. You can even activate two corners at the same time if knowledge can complement your creativity. Then you'd redesign the wisdom corner too.

Maybe you still need to find your true self. Then you'll need to focus on the center of the room. This space helps us find our roots and be truthful and gentle with our minds and souls. Do you wish to be humbler? Why not focus on the bottom-right corner instead? Change the room as many times as you want. Try not to have too many negative elements in your space either. For example, have two yins and one yang element. Don't have three yang spaces activated at once. Keep your command position in mind too. You don't need to be seated in the spaces you've activated. Just make sure you're facing the doorway diagonally. The same applies to bedrooms, kitchens, and family rooms if you can move them about.

Your workstation, desk, stove, or bed must be in the command position to benefit from the Feng Shui energy flow. Beds are often placed strategically against the wall and facing the door because the bedroom is a vulnerable place. Sleep ignites creativity, so make sure your bedroom is mapped correctly. There's only one rule you must follow when using Feng Shui in your home. Never exceed three energy enhancement centers simultaneously in the same room. This will cause higher energy vibrations to form negative collisions again. Decorate and explore three principles at a time, and nothing more.

Then you can move on to the next room. The more the energy flows throughout your home, the better every area of your life that correlates to creativity will become. Another secret to enhancing your Bagua mapping is to place your most prized artwork in the fame space in the top-center of the room. This needn't add to your three choices for that room. You're simply amplifying your work that already enhanced your reputation. It's called strutting your stuff.

I'm going to give you a few examples to inspire your Feng Shui. The goals will differ and the rooms will change. Your greatest goal is to balance the flow of energy and remove stagnant or dangerous energies from your home, and especially from your creation station. Your creative genius will explode when you get this right.

Room Sample for Creative Block

Choosing the creative space is the most obvious choice here. Complement this space with the metal element and white or gray coloration. Why not place a small white, metallic, round table under a new photo you took of the ocean? Water acts as a secondary supporting element to creativity. You can also use mild and gentle yellows that aren't bright. It must be closer to white than it is to yellow.

Heck, place a round tub chair against the wall, and hang an abstract painting of circles. Place a circular-shaped lampshade that burns white. Finally, take anything you've created yourself. It can be from your professional medium or it can be a random doodle you drew. This magnifies the creative energy in this space, and using a child-like doodle could also prompt your inner child to come out.

Enhancing your wisdom space might also remove creative blocks because you find inspiration when you're looking for more answers. Place a small end table in the bottom-right of your room and find a dark blue vase to plant something in. Earth is the grounded element and you can plant something in the soil to use it.

Finally, activate the center space with a light brown square rug to ground your truth in the room. Being true to yourself will help you overcome a creative block too. Just make sure that the color is as light as possible so that it doesn't clash with the very mild yellow in your creativity corner and the dark blue vase.

Room Sample for Creative Self-Growth

I'd start with the wisdom corner for this one. Make a hand-imprint of yourself with some dark blue paint and frame it in a square frame. Take glue and spread some dirt on the frame itself to add the earth element. Hanging this in the wisdom corner will do.

Secondly, activate the wealth principle to seek abundance in the top-left corner. Abundance displays growth so you'll be using a little foresight here. This is a fun one because its element is wood. Wood sculptors can create something for this area or you can place a small, rectangular wooden table in the corner. Purchase a purple runner for the table, one that complements the dark blue in the bottom-left corner of the room. It can be a lighter shade of purple.

Lastly, self-growth is also enhanced through the center principle to always desire self-improvement. A rug would work fine here but I'd go with a new light shade. Look for something earthy, rugged, and square. Use a color globe in an extremely mild yellow. It should be closer to white or beige to stop the upset of the purple and blue colors in the corners.

Room Sample for Being Unstoppably True to Your Creative Genius

This sample can be used elsewhere. I'll use the family room for this one because it's recommended to enhance your family and relationships when your spouse or kids are unsupportive of your desires. Use the lightest shades of each color to make sure they don't clash.

Start with the family corner and place a rectangular wooden table in it with a honeydew green overthrow. This will be in the center-left of the room. Place a rectangular wooden frame above this. The picture can be of you and your family visiting a place in spring. Remember that spring is the season for family. This principle also encourages new beginnings.

The partnership corner in the top-right represents love and relationships. Use patient white, which is a super-light shade of pink, and create a sketch of two hearts overlapping each other on the patient white background you choose. It can be a flat canvas or framed in a square shape. The partnership principle is also about earthing yourself in self-care, so add a pot plant with dirt in it. The pot must also be as light pink as possible.

Finally, focus on the helpful people principle in the bottom-right corner of the room. Place a round gray floor lamp in this corner. This principle can also help you follow your head while you're catering to the needs of your heart from the picture in the partnership corner.

Room Sample for Sleep

Our minds are busy while we're asleep, so you want to enhance your brain at night. Place your bed in the command position which would either be against the right-side wall to face the door or it will be immediately diagonal to the doorway.

Right-sided placement helps you already work on the creative corner that can stimulate energy flow while you sleep. Therefore, use white or gray linen and complement it with a circular mirror placed above the headboard. Remember that wall-hangings must be high. The mirror is also reflective of your ideas and adds a metallic color. Placing your bed against the furthest wall would require red linen and something from summer vacation to hang above your headboard. This gives you two options for bed placements already.

You can use the center self-principle to ground yourself in your sleep by placing a brown rug in the center of the room. This would be the option for red linen, but white linen would rather be complemented by activating the partnership principle in the top-right corner with some pink flair. White and pink work well together anyway. Hang a picture of a beautiful bunch of pink flowers and it will look great with your linen.

Finally, complement the red linen by activating the top-left corner with a wooden dresser to create abundant sleep. White linen and pink flowers will go well with a light beige and square rug in the center of the room to activate your well-being while you sleep.

Feng Shui is an incredible skill and you'll have tons of fun creating new rooms. You also don't have to use three principles with every room because not every color fits with another one. Focus on shapes or elements if the colors seem off. Start redesigning your home today and you'll be managing your unstoppable creativity from the outside in no time.

Chapter 5:

How to Prompt Your

Creative Genius on

Command

You have your creative space now and you've learned about driving internal creativity to become unstoppable, but sometimes, you still hit a brick wall while you're soaking up the energy in your Feng Shui space. Sometimes, you still can't find the next sentence to flow into another chapter, or you can't piece your images together to create a new concept. Harnessing your creativeness and asserting your new title won't always guarantee ingenuity at the drop of a hat. You must learn how to enter the invaluable flow state to command your creativity at your whim. Tapping into it, honing it, and exerting the flow state is how you rush through those mental blocks when you feel stumped.

Understanding the Flow State

The flow state is a powerful creative tool that helps you smash the brick wall in front of you whenever you need to resonate with creative genius. This is where the "trick your brain" techniques start because let's face it, even when you've done everything right, a mountain can still drop onto your path. Mental blocks are common for creative people and this mountain can often seem insurmountable. Your ultimate goal is to reach a flow state and become so masterful at using it that mountains are moved on your command.

What is the Flow State?

First introduced by Psychologist Mihaly Csikszentmihalyi in his book *Flow State*, the concept is to become so immersed in what you're doing that everything else takes a distant back seat (Csikszentmihalyi, 2016). You enter a new, deeper level of focus that can even bring about a state of ecstasy, much like the piano player who got lost in his musical creation. Therefore, the flow state is simply the art of already being happy with what you're doing while having a purpose-driven mission you want to achieve.

You know what you want and need to do to get from one point of your creative journey to the next. You aren't focused on the outcome alone. You're intertwining yourself with every aspect of the journey.

Being keenly focused on a project that you're passionate about, and that means something deeper to you, is how you switch over to another state of mind and ultimately get lost in the moment. The flow state is commonly seen in high-performing individuals who play chess, run marathons, and even surgeons.

It helps you remove yourself from the distractions around you and concentrate on what you're doing right now. Distractions are often to blame for removing our creative mind from the present moment and making us feel blocked. One secret to the flow state is that it's more common in challenging situations because we need full engagement. We can only be happy when we're pursuing a project that's complex and requires us to use our full potential.

Csikszentmihalyi explains one important key in his book. The human brain is only capable of processing 120 bits of information at once and that's why we need to apply every bit to our creative concentration. You know that you lose focus when someone talks to you and then you can't even remember which direction your brush strokes were following anymore. Processing words can already use between 60 and 80 bits of information, not leaving you with much for your canvas.

Your processing capacity also helps you understand why challenging yourself with a more complex idea is better than trying to find flow in a menial, coasting project. You can't reach the flow state if there's too much room to allow distractions to waste information processing. As long as you're passionate about what you're doing, using every bit of information available for processing will help you reach the fulfilled state of flow. Feeling fulfilled will motivate you to keep going.

The flow state enables multiple benefits. This magical but psychological state of mind will drive the intrinsic rewards inside of you to keep you motivated and engaged. There are many benefits to the flow state besides tricking your mind into doing your bidding by feeding it with intrinsic rewards. Remember that intrinsic rewards will help your new pulse connections multiply and strengthen as well, creating new habits. Who wouldn't want creativity on command as a habit?

Other benefits include a higher level of concentration, which helps you exert higher-quality work. You have a sense of clarity about where you're going and how to get there. This also doubles the benefits of your step-by-step goal settings. The flow state encourages you to become so immersed in your work that stress, distractions, and self-doubt vanish too. Finally, reaching the state of fulfillment and ultimate joy will drive your happiness levels through the roof.

You won't be worried about your work anymore. You're giving it everything you have and expressing every quality you possess. Your focus will peak at new heights and you won't be self-conscious anymore. In fact, entering the flow state is where you lose track of time because you're so engaged in what you're doing. Time will either slow down or you'll lose track of it entirely. Being so deeply involved in your work also allows you to track your performance on the go.

Your skills will be tested to new extremes, and you can always acknowledge new skills you need if you don't manage to reach the flow state. You won't easily get into it if you're too challenged either. Choose projects and ideas that challenge your full potential, but also cause you to learn new skills in order to reach the state. Some people are capable of reaching it when they apply their full focus to learning new skills.

Try activating the flow state by triggering your limits and use it to learn new skills if you're lacking some. You can always return to the flow state by reaching for more challenging journeys if your journey is too easy. Easy has never activated intrinsic rewards and that's why you can't self-actualize or find purposeful fulfillment through taking the easy road. The flow state requires you to step out of the safe zone and into one where you're connected to your work.

Tapping the Flow

I'm not going to lie and say that this is easy, effortless, and anyone can do it because it requires practice, intention, and determination. Well, anyone can do it as long as they're determined enough. The flow state will increase your productivity and creativity simply because you'll be so focused and engaged that nothing will stand between you and your desires. The first and most important reason to reach the flow state is that you must desire your outcome deeper than anything you've ever wanted.

It must align with your passions and give you purpose, meaning, and core ambitions in life. Is the book you're writing important to you? Is the painting you're working on more meaningful than every predecessor? If so, you're ready. There are certain triggers or methods that help you reach the flow state other than passion.

The first trigger is to choose work that you love and that means something to your long-term career as an artist. Don't choose the easy route, instead, challenge yourself to ignite the most important passions you have. The project must also be challenging enough to use your full capacity, but not so hard that you can't reach the flow state. Remember that you can always learn new skills and train yourself to flow with the learning process.

The second trigger is to remove all distractions from your flow space because they're your worst enemy. They'll tug at your attention span and leave you without enough space to reach your full potential in the project you're busy with. External distractions could even include people talking in the next room. Get sound-blocking headphones and prevent this from using your capacity. Oxford University recommends 10 to 15 minutes of intensive focus without distractions to reach the flow state (Nakamura & Csikszentmihalyi, 2009).

Your phone, emails, and anything else in your environment that isn't directly needed for your work are classified as external distractions. It can take you up to 25 minutes to return to the flow state once you've lost it. Internal distractions can be just as counterproductive. You might have thoughts, worries, or emotions bouncing about your mind. Take care of them by journaling, through meditation, and spending allocated time on emotional acceptance strategies.

The third trigger is to find your biological peak time (BPT). It's hard to focus when you're low on energy, so you need to determine when you're at your peak. Focus and concentration also require energy. You can only enter the flow state in your BPT, so it's best to take a genuine break before trying. Many people prefer working on the most challenging projects early in the day. Other people allocate an hour right after waking up. However, you can also take the break by meditating first or doing something relaxing that doesn't involve electronic distractions. So, no Facebook, YouTube, or Netflix before entering the flow.

There are four types of rest you can implement to ensure that your mind has enough energy to continue in the flow state. Meditation helps you obtain mental rest because you're focused on your internal state, desires, and goals instead of your smartphone. Social rest also works because you can spend some time with friends to re-energize your mind again. Spiritual rest also works when you're in nature or spend time silently in a place of worship. Physical rest is achieved through sleep, but you can also lay in a hot bath, go for a walk, or join a yoga class to stretch and restore your muscles.

The fourth trigger for the flow state is to fill your mind with the correct enhancements. You're not distracting your mind, but rather filling it with sound waves that help your brain reach its peak performance stage. Classical, trance, and techno music has a repetitive beat that helps you keep a rhythm when you're focused. Choose faster rhythms to keep your mind awake with a funky beat. I often use music without lyrics though or I find myself distracted. Also, use the repeat function so that the music becomes part of your flow. Don't change songs every five minutes; keep the same beat going.

The fifth trigger is another one that aligns itself with your goal-setting strategies. Be specific about what your project entails today. You can't hone your focus if you don't know what you're focusing on. The flow state is about singling out a creative project and concentrating solely on it. Multitasking isn't part of being in the flow. Your outcome and journey must be clear because clarity will help your brain stay focused.

The sixth trigger is to choose something challenging enough. You become bored and apathetic if you are too relaxed. You'll feel like you're more in control if the challenge causes some worry and concern. However, projects that ignite anxiety will create flow because they arouse your brain's alertness. Make sure you choose projects that wake your brain up, but they can't hold you back by being too complicated.

Trigger seven is as simple as supplying the brain with water. A healthy brain is a thinking brain. You can't maintain focus when your brain doesn't get what it needs. Remember that brain health is the key to creativity. After all, the brain is also about 75% water and couldn't survive without this valuable commodity.

Trigger eight reminds you to practice your flow state. You need to practice concentrating long enough to get lost in the moment. Commit to your project if you've allocated an hour to work on it. Don't switch between projects or wander off halfway through it.

The ninth trigger is to reward times you reach the flow state. Intrinsic rewards are at work, but give yourself an appropriate reward for getting lost in your music, sketches, paintings, and writing. Don't give yourself an hour-long break every time you finish 30 minutes of flow, but spend 10 minutes acknowledging your success.

Finally, trick your mind into using specified cues to know that it's time to work now. Create a mental cue every time you want to enter the flow state and practice it each time. You might use an affirmation to get your brain ready. You could say: "I'm entering the flow of the creation in front of me now and I shall enjoy every moment of it." You can also use other cues, such as having a cup of tea before sitting down. Do anything to trick your brain into knowing that flow time has arrived.

The flow state is an incredible experience. Have you noticed how your worries dissipate when you're so immersed in a project that you don't even realize the entire day has evaporated? You feel your hands being interconnected with the cold clay as it becomes smoother and smoother while you guide it. You're the conductor of the musical symphony we call the flow state. Your direct focus is what turns a bunch of screeching instruments into a flow of harmonious sound waves that strike the core of everyone in the observation hall.

Mindful Flow

Mindfulness and the flow state have a few things in common. They both require you to focus on precisely what you're busy within the present moment. You're not trapped in thoughts of tomorrow and disappointments from yesteryear. It's just you and the creation in your hands. Nothing else exists in the flow moment besides you and your art. Mindfulness teaches you to focus keenly on the task at hand and enjoy every moment of it because the present moment is the only one that exists. Your separation from distractions is also a mindful practice, and having a higher sense of control is connected to the flow state and mindfulness.

Other factors shared by the two methods are that both improve your attention as long as you continue practicing them. Mindfulness even teaches you to train your focus on what you desire so that you can reach a flow state easier. The immediate feedback and performance tracking are also part of both practices. You're so engulfed in what you're doing that you're constantly tracking your performance, and this gives you immediate feedback. Both options also help you enjoy every part of what you're doing. Being in the present moment is where you experience everything through your senses. You enjoy your food more when you mindfully partake in it with every sense you have. The flow state also allows you to use all your senses to be one with your project.

Anything mindful will instigate a flow state and allow you to get lost in your projects. This includes reading and writing, partaking in hobbies, being engulfed in art, and exercising. Teach yourself to be mindful of every little task you complete, even making dinner. Talk to yourself and explain the steps you're taking. Smell the spices and taste the gravy. Listen to the meat cracking in the pan as you focus on every sensory stimulation you can perceive from a task as simple as making dinner. Be mindful of anything you do, and immersing yourself into tasks mindfully will help you practice your flow state.

Meditation and journaling will train your brain to use the flow state, but there's a newer mindful method of switching your brain over. The autonomous sensory meridian response (ASMR) is stimulated by certain visual and audio triggers that ignite the flow state (Barrat & Davis, 2015). Certain tapping sounds can spark tingling sensations in the brain and wake it up for higher concentration. You can listen to meridian tapping sounds while you work or you can learn to tap yourself while in a meditation state. Ambient background noise and whispering have the same effects as tapping sounds and can help you reach the flow state if you wear headphones while sitting at your creation station.

Mindfulness teaches you to become one with focused sensory stimuli, and any action, activity, or experience where you insert your senses fully will work. Even completing a Sudoku puzzle while intentionally focusing on it is a way of being mindful. There are numerous ways of establishing a mindful connection to your project after you practice it in your daily life. Don't just walk through the park. Listen, feel, see, taste, and smell everything as you pass it. Become fully engulfed in every step you take.

Top 20 Tricks to Spark the Flow State

I've compiled a list of 20 tricks that help me ignite inspiration on command when I'm feeling blocked. Remember to be mindful of every method and use your senses to fully experience it.

Trick One: Start Journaling

This sounds simple enough, but you should journal every morning for 10 minutes after waking up. Your mind is fresh at this point and everything you write comes from the deepest parts of your creative genius. Don't worry about what you'll write. Heck, jot down your dreams or a sweet memory from yesterday. You might just find inspiration when you aren't looking for it. You can also keep a dream diary to record all the experiences you have while asleep. Many artists find inspiration in their dreams because it's where the imagination comes out to play.

Trick Two: Gather Groupies

Creativity and art can be lonely journeys, and you're supposed to surround yourself with an inspiring community while inspiring them too. Have three groupies available to call when you feel slumped. Go for a coffee and speak to them about their art. They can give you ideas that slipped your mind. Share ideas and inspiration by meeting up with your creative groupies frequently.

Trick Three: Change Perspectives

Often, we find new inspiration when we stop looking at the current painting in front of us. Don't dawdle forever, but go for a walk, throw a towel over your canvas, or close your laptop while you do something spontaneous. Do something mindful for 15 minutes and return to the project you're busy with. However, try not to sit on Facebook for this time unless you're browsing through posts by fellow artists to see what ideas you can get inspiration from.

Trick Four: Carry a Notebook

Inspiration doesn't always hit when we expect it, and you're as capable of forgetting ideas as I am of forgetting an amazing quote I never recorded. Take your notebook everywhere and don't care if people wonder what you're doing when you pull it out. Inspiration can be found in everything, everywhere, at any time. Don't be afraid to visually record your inspiration either. Snap photos or doodle something you see that strikes a core inside of you. Take photos of everything and everyone.

Trick Five: Explore

Leave the comfort of your studio and visit a bustling mall, coffee shop, or an event nearby. Watch people go about their days and take notes of what they're doing. Be mindfully descriptive in your notes too. Don't be afraid to be the weirdo at the coffee shop who's watching the world around you. Wear sunglasses if you don't want to stand out as a weirdo. You can also travel to new places and observe new faces. Remember that ideas come from experiences and your inspiration will dry up like a prune if you aren't experiencing new things.

Countless artists use their travels for inspiration. Changing your environment can make you see things that weren't available to your artistic perception before. You also don't have to travel alone. Invite one of your artistic groupies along so that you can share ideas as you encounter new environments. The most important rule of this trick is that you don't only observe. Get involved and experience places where you've never been before. You might not be inspired right away, but you could find new concepts when you partake in a memorable meditation session next week.

Trick Six: Explore Yourself

Find a quiet spot and meditate so that you can reconnect with the person inside of you. You want to awaken the inner child and allow your emotions to ignite inspiration. Close your eyes and become one with your thoughts and emotions. Let your thoughts walk in steps. Start with what you need to do right now. You need to find inspiration. So, how are you going to do this? Keep your eyes closed as you simply follow your train of thoughts. Allow them to wander in your silent space if this is what they do. They might wander to something you haven't noticed yet. Suddenly, you're thinking about the Halloween party at your office and what costume you'll wear. Permit this thought because it's also sparking creativity. Any creative spark will set off larger flames if you welcome them.

Trick Seven: Memorable Meditation

Spend 10 minutes in a memorable meditation session. Listen to a guided session on Headspace or you can just close your eyes and follow your breathing. Think of a time you were happy and determined. It needn't be about your creative side. Maybe you remember a holiday where you visited a new place. Focus on your emotions as you allow the memory to play like a movie. Keep an eye on what you're doing to make you feel elated. Try to remember the sounds, smells, tastes, sights, and feelings of this memory.

You can also use photos for visual cues if you aren't great at meditating yet. I recommend that you learn how to meditate because it requires practice. Use photos or speak to friends and family while you reminisce about happy memories. Don't focus deeply on negative memories unless you're looking for the appropriate inspiration. Our emotions can trigger incredible inspiration, whether we're anxious or elated. Commit to memorable sessions where you can use the driving force of emotions to see details you might've missed before.

Trick Eight: Become an Avid Reader

Finding inspiration is sometimes as simple as reading a novel or listening to an intriguing fiction story on Audible. The way good writers paint a picture in your mind while you read is incredibly powerful. It could teach you how to paint images in your mind by using your imagination more often. Fiction writers use their creativeness from the first page where they introduce an unknown place and create characters that are sometimes out of this world.

Trick Nine: Dare Yourself

Leave the comfort of your creation station and become curious, adventurous, and daring. Try new activities and push your limits to the maximum so that you can use your full capacity to focus hard enough on the flow state. You don't have to even dare yourself to do things similar to your medium. Try new things and learn new skills. Take a painting class if you're a writer, or learn to play an instrument if you're a sculptor.

Trick Ten: Follow Your Instincts

Our instincts are the inner-child speaking to us, so if you feel like taking a trip to an exposé in the next town, do it. Don't miss opportunities because that isn't being mindful. The same applies to something that doesn't seem right. Are your instincts telling you that the painting you're busy with is the worst idea you've ever had? Listen to your inner-child and throw it away.

Trick Eleven: Use Your RAS

The reticular activating system will kick in if you simply choose to start. Start with your project now unless you're headed out to collect inspiration. As you see it taking shape, so shall inspiration be motivated. Starting a new chapter is always daunting for me. My fear lessens once I see the words forming sentences and the story taking shape. Starting will always be the hardest part of anything in life. However, the words gain momentum and so does my motivation. Besides, it's easier to go back and make small changes than it is to start in the first place.

Trick Twelve: Prioritizing Simplicities

Your project must be challenging, but not your preparation for it. Make sure that all your art supplies, laptop, brushes, canvas, clay, and whatever you use in your medium are easily accessible to you. You want to start fast and make distractions hard to begin with. Unplug your television and stick it in the closet so that it's a huge job just to binge-watch Netflix. Rather have your creation station ready to start at any moment and make every distraction as complex as possible.

Trick Thirteen: Permit Yourself to Doodle

Doodling isn't only for kids and it's certainly not reserved for sketch artists. Sometimes, our ideas have no words yet, or they don't have an exact shape at first. Have another notebook where you simply doodle the craziest things that pop into your mind. They don't need to have any meaning, explanation, or structure. Creative geniuses can see beyond what the regular person can, and that's how they renew ideas and connect dots that no one else did.

Allocate one large sketch pad page daily and doodle any shapes, forms, colors, sizes, and concoctions on the same page for 24 hours. Study this page in the morning when you have a fresh mind and see if it makes any sense to you. After all, those are all thoughts, inspirational ideas, and emotions you've doodled into scribbles. Try to piece them together like a puzzle now.

Trick Fourteen: Surprise Yourself with New Ventures

No artist has ever become famous by staying in their studio and not partaking in the world. Try new things, even if it's a different medium to yours. Attend new classes and enjoy new hobbies that also offer creative flair. Most people can be creative in various areas, but they restrict themselves to one or two. You don't have to partake in them fully either. Attend concerts and theater to observe the show and gain inspiration.

Best of all, sign up for a real challenge. Enter your short novel in a contest or showcase your painting at the local gallery to win a prize. Not only do you see other people's work, but you're also challenging yourself to create something more meaningful than other artists. Don't let failure deter you and don't let it make you judge yourself. However, winning a prize for your work could help you overcome mental blocks.

Trick Fifteen: Create Something for Yourself

Why not create a piece of work for your eyes alone if you're feeling blocked? Don't hesitate because hesitation kills inspiration. Instead, put your time to better use while you're looking for inspiration for your big ideas. Paint yourself a picture, write a short article to summarize tips about your medium, or create something homemade for your Feng Shui environment. Creative spark will lead to more creativity, as long as you're exercising it often enough.

Trick Sixteen: Study Inspiring People Religiously

Keep your eyes on the ball as you study people who've made it. Remember not to envy them but only to take inspiration from your mentors or previously successful people in your medium. Look at other mediums too because a painter can inspire a writer and vice versa. What did they do to make it? Don't be afraid to approach them and ask either. Listen to their stories and follow their artistic climb on the ladder of success because this sparks powerful inspiration.

Trick Seventeen: Never Dismiss Ideas

Every idea you have is worth something, even if it's for your Feng Shui mapping. Don't dismiss ideas and keep every hint of inspiration you note down in a box. This box will fill with many unusable ideas, but you won't believe how many inspirational concepts come from it when you've been filling it for three months. You can then piece together numerous inspirational ideas to create one explosion of unstoppable ingenuity. Your inspiration notebook must also be thrown in this box along with your doodles so that you can piece the puzzle together when you need inspiration after hitting a brick wall.

Trick Eighteen: Browse Consumer Insights

Pinterest is a good place to see what people like and how you can improve on what they already have. All you need is one keyword and you can find an endless ocean of ideas in a visual format. Not having a keyword isn't a problem either. Use HubSpot or Portent to generate ideas, topics, and keywords when you're feeling like a blank canvas. Otherwise, don't be surprised at what you find when you enter the words "tree art" into Pinterest.

Trick Nineteen: Research Failed Ideas

This sounds horrid but remember that creative geniuses take ideas that no one else used to invent new understandings, and they rework it until it becomes understood by the current evolution. Go back a few decades or even 100 years and dig up artwork that was a complete miss. Now, spend time with these ideas and see if and how you can improve them. This is what scientists do daily.

Trick Twenty: Be Curious Enough to See Other Views

This is the biggest trick that guarantees a spark of ingenuity when it's most needed! Creative can't exist unless you question what's in front of you from every angle. Digest information through any medium that you don't agree with. This will ignite emotions inside of you that you didn't even know existed. Emotions are the precursor for the greatest artwork in history. Your emotions will run high while you try to defend the opposite of what the work expresses and the energy that will flood out of you is none other than the peak of creative genius.

Ultimately, you're going to have to come up with multiple strategies to switch the light back on for you over time. Not every trick works for everyone and you won't be able to implement every one of them when you need to, but keep experimenting with various tricks to overcome your mental blocks. Embrace the fact that not every trick will work and try each one until you have your working option. You want the trick to resonate with you just as you become immersed in activities and projects.

Chapter 6:

The Art of Letting Go

And still, even after putting all this valuable information to use, you might hit another brick wall. You should never beat yourself up because it's okay, it happens to all of us. You may have generated your own blocks by trying too hard. We get caught up in the need to be creative and often forget that creativity is a gentle flow that can't be forced. Sometimes, we simply need to let go. Letting go is the final tool to ensure that you find your spark again.

What "Letting Go" Means

Letting go comes with negative connotations, but it's a skillful decision that makes life flow the way it should. It's not the simple act of releasing a person, project, or desire. It's a collection of actions and decisions that open your life to a universal direction. Sometimes, you can't let go even if you want to, or you can let go but you don't feel like it. The negative idea behind letting go is often seen in relationships and goals. Someone dies and everyone tells you to let go. Someone leaves and everyone echoes the same line. A project doesn't go the way you want it to and everyone tells you to stop wasting your time.

Letting go is a decision that things won't return or be the same if they do. In a way, it allows you to hone your survival skills. It's a painful and beautiful process that often comes with a price. You can afford the cost but you need to earn it. Hope can fade momentarily when you let go, but it will vanish entirely if you don't let go. Letting go might come with some setbacks, negative emotions, and feelings of disappointment, but it helps you find your true self as well. Life is the most unpredictable experience and holding on to directions we aren't meant to follow will only hurt us more.

It's like forgiving someone, and sometimes, this person is yourself. It doesn't mean that you messed things up for good. You forgive yourself for not being the person you thought you were supposed to be. Letting go of hurtful feelings can help you move away from them, but you'll only ruminate on the consequences if you remain ashamed of not being good or creative enough. Life is unpredictable, but it flows and you can only flow with it if you're prepared to let go of directions that weren't intended for you.

Sometimes, you must release the person you thought you had to be and allow life to guide you to the incredible, unstoppable artist you're meant to be. Letting go is a way of challenging yourself to do things differently, and experience different things. You're asking life to help you and redirect your artistry into an avenue previously dismissed. This doesn't mean that you must change mediums; it means that you need to go with the flow and open your mind to new ways of doing things. Pursue the unknown instead of hiding in a shell of familiarity.

Become positive in negative situations, be confident when things look dreary, and harness your strengths in weak moments. Letting go is accepting life and its unpredictability so that you can recognize things that can't be changed. It also helps you look at things differently in order to change what you can. Let go so that you can know what's worth fighting for and what isn't.

It's easy to become overwhelmed when life doesn't go the way we want it to, but often, we end up in a better place when we allow the flow to move us. You can't let go of something you haven't experienced before, so this means that you've experienced magical creativity in the past and simply need to let go so that life can direct you back to what you're meant to become. Resisting letting go can be more harmful than persevering in some cases. Trying too hard won't help you to create something amazing.

Artists can't become their greatest versions if they follow conventional rules. Unstoppable creatives must learn, unlearn, and relearn daily to keep the creative flow moving and to create true art. You can't let go of conventional ideas if you aren't prepared to learn what they are and commit to changing them.

Another reason why many of us need to let go is that we don't always have the resources we intend to use for our creations, and this causes a mental block. Let go of the fancy paints and expensive materials you need to create something and look around you. Life will always give you the materials needed, but you won't see them if your eyes are locked onto the wrong ideas.

Sometimes, we simply need to let go of the way we think. Reactivating the flow can be achieved by gaining new perspectives and questioning conventional methods. Collaboration is one way of letting go by allowing someone else to help you see past the blocks.

Refusing to let go of old ideas that aren't working can also prevent you from starting your projects. Your mind is strapped to the ideas you desire, and you're forgetting about the flow that life is using to guide you to greater things.

You could also be holding yourself back by not letting go because you might be focused on your average skills and not your strengths. Being unstoppably creative means that we must use our greatest strengths and perfect them to establish the connections in our brains to overcome mental blocks. Think of it as chasing the wrong desires. Why not use the strengths you have to chase the right desires instead?

You can't be true to yourself or eccentric as most famous artists are if you're holding yourself back either. There are more artists today than there were in Picasso's time, and you won't be achieving anything if you won't let go of ideas that prevent you from being unique.

Finally, some ideas are just rotten to their core. It happens to all of us, anyone can create a painting or write a laughably boring book that makes people cringe. This is where the self-forgiveness comes into play. You won't move away from this harmful shame if you can't let go. What happened has already happened and ruminating on the failure isn't going to change it. It will conjure negative thoughts and emotions to prevent you from expressing your creativeness.

Please do me a favor and research a book called *The Missionary Position: Mother Teresa in Theory and Practice* by Christopher Hitchens. The image of Mother Theresa on this cover is perfect; however, the name is the problem here. A magnificent book, written well and thoughtfully presented, was ruined by an overlooked title. The missionary position is a favorite sexual coupling and no one would ever connect Mother Teresa to that. Unfortunately, the book hit the shelves and the author was shamed for the misconception on the cover.

This is one of the numerous examples where a simple mistake turned a great book into a laughable creation. It happens to every creative person and all you can do is forgive yourself, hold no grudge, and let go of the mistake. Letting go is how you return to the flow after you've experienced a setback.

Knowing When to Let Go

Recognizing when to let go is another story, though. It's one of those easier said than done paradoxes. The problem is that we start overthinking, holding a grudge against ourselves for not achieving what we thought we had to, and we ultimately try too hard. Overthinking and trying too hard can be the death of creativity, though. Being productive doesn't always mean that you're creative when you try to force an idea. Art flows freely and it becomes a mistake when you're forcing it. Writers know that no one wants to read something that's forced. The words need to flow naturally and so does any form of art.

Readers, listeners, and observers are also repelled by work that tries too hard. Your work is for sale if you're an artist by career, but no one likes a sales pitch when they want to enjoy an artful expression. Also, we tend to use conventional methods to attract sales, and there's nothing unique about selling the same product that everyone else does. Forced ideas become contrived and quite painful because no one wants to embrace the expression you've shared. Passion is missing in your expression when it's forced.

Never assume that producing more is better than producing passionate quality that resonates with people. You'll need to return to your flow to show your passion in your work again. This can only be done by letting go. Observers of art want to see the real you, the original idea behind your work, and not some contrived enforcement that lacks emotion. Humans don't like an idea that begs for attention. People will always want what is harder to possess. Make your work unique in quality where everyone desires it without you needing a sales pitch. You only want the right attention for your creations, and that's why you need to learn about the reasons for letting go.

First, your brain is always in defense mode. This is a biological process that the brain uses when it perceives threats (DiSalvo, 2013). The limbic system, including the hyperactive, emotional amygdala, is home to the fight or flight response. The body's desire to survive in this world means that this response is triggered in milliseconds, which is a good thing, but it's also a bad thing. It all depends on the context when it activates. This center of your brain is always looking for more threats to defend you against, but hitting a mental block in your creativity isn't a real threat. It can seem so when you're permanently in defense mode and hyper-reactive to the world around you.

Remember that you need time to enter your flow state, and you certainly have a creative problem if your brain is preventing this because it remains in the fight or flight mode. You need to let go to overcome this mode.

Self-efficacy is the faith we have in ourselves and our abilities and it's another reason for letting go. It's more than confidence because we trust that we can overcome an obstacle or find a new idea to create something amazing. But, doubt can begin snowballing into your habits and you can lose your confidence in your abilities. Letting go of failures is the only way you can reverse the snowball effect so that you're learning from past mistakes instead of doubting yourself after making them.

It's difficult to stop thinking about your past failures because the brain plays them back like a movie every time it feels threatened by another trigger that reminds it of past failures. The governing scenes conjured by your subconscious mind goes one of two ways. You either fear trying again, or you let the images go and move forward. Shame is a terrible, frightening emotion and it can prevent you from being creative if you hold on to it.

Some answers also won't be revealed until evolutionary understanding catches up to it, accept this. Let go of ideas that don't make sense yet. Yes, creatives need to be curious, but they also need to let go of ideas that aren't fathomable yet.

The fear of being creative can also disrupt your flow. Ingenuity is a disruptive force that's volatile, presumptuous, and is capable of dismantling your previous ideas. It can undermine your expectations if you're expecting too much. This is why creativity appears threatening to the brain because it isn't rainbows, lollipops, and unicorns. It can be a mighty force that consumes your mind. Your brain might fear it and react. Sometimes, we need to let go of the thought that our entire life must be creative. Rather decide how much creativity you can handle before you succumb to the fight or flight response.

Creativity isn't always a sudden splash of tangible creation either. It often collects subconsciously in the background, and we can misinterpret the ideas, especially when it suddenly pops into our conscious mind as a collective that we can't interpret without letting go first. You need enough time to interpret the ideas; it's difficult to understand them without the chunks of time needed. Our minds can't understand the flurry of noise in the background when this idea finally surfaces.

Preventing the background noise from overwhelming you is as simple as writing everything down that moves through your mind. You must let go of ideas onto paper until you can return to a quieter background. Remember that we don't allow opportunities to slip, but sometimes, we must let go of them so that we can clear our minds again. Putting them on paper ensures that you don't throw them away.

Sadly, the brain also becomes so overwhelmed with stress that it numbs the creativity inside of you with a flurry of distractions. Simply, this is another description of the mental block. However, the brain will try to distract you anyway it can. Some people are prone to alcohol and narcotics to drown the noise, but the brain is smart. It can also drown your creativity under the disguise of Netflix, Facebook, smartphones, and anything that deters you from being creative. This is a major reason for letting go of the swarming ideas in your mind.

Another way our brains retaliate against the flow state we wish to rejoin is when we stop looking for inspiration from other artists and the environment. Creatives cannot survive without inspiration, and avoiding it means that you need to let go quickly. You can only combat this retaliation by increasing your exposure to inspiring people.

The brain is a powerful organ but it can also cripple your creativity. The biggest secret here is that you need to stop trying so hard. Stop trying to be creative when your brain is reacting like this. Stop forcing yourself to reach epiphanies and create magnanimous art when your brain needs to simply let go for a while. Letting go doesn't mean that you must push creativity aside; it means that you must take a step back before you can move forward. Remember that you're creative and your creativity won't vanish if you take a break. There will be days you can't control the ingenuity and that's okay, you must let it go.

The faster you hit a brick wall, the more you get hurt. Slow down and be gentle with yourself. Be gentle to the brain that's only trying to defend you. Your ideas aren't gone. They aren't invisible. You're simply allowing the brain to recuperate. Conscious thoughts require energy and so does creativity. Step back and allow ideas, concepts, and new creations to come to you. Don't hunt them when your mind needs a break. You'll only be forcing your creativity and pushing out low-quality work. Start by remembering what brought creation to your mind in the first place. Return to this primitive state and let go of the urgent need to produce, create, and enforce.

Managing the Fears

Letting go allows life to bring inspiration to you while you're in a block. However, the brain is busy and it will always be easier to say it than apply it. That's why you need to be ready for the stress that comes from letting go and then waiting for your desires to come to you. Being mindful will help you during this time. Mindfulness-based stress reduction (MBSR) programs have been used to combat general anxiety disorder (GAD) successfully (Hoge et al., 2013). Become mindful and you'll be one step closer to reconnecting with your flow state. Adopt mindful attitudes by applying new rules to your life.

First, look for the silver lining in every cloud, whether it's dark or not. There will be bad days and you'll feel down during your block period. Experience the day by looking for good moments, even when the day seems impossible. Mindfulness is being present at all times, and you can only enjoy life in the present. Use your senses to experience everything or you'll be missing the silver lining if you're looking at the problem-manifesting ground.

Become accepting of life and its unpredictability. You're not superhuman and can't avoid every problem. You can't fix everything that breaks. You can't force creativity when the stream has paused. You have limits and there's nothing more powerful than accepting what you can do.

Always live in the present because you'll be missing out if you don't. Anxious thoughts have a way of pulling us into past mistakes and future concerns. Live for now and enjoy every minute as best as you can. Who knows? Life might pull you back into the flow, but you'll miss the slipway if you're looking in the rear-view mirror.

Let go of your worries and allow yourself to be surprised. Continue wanting to learn more and being curious. People who pretend to know everything will never be open to new ideas if they're closing their minds. Don't prove yourself to anyone. You know what your current position is and where your destination lies.

Surrender to life and allow the flow to grab you again. Don't fight against change because you never know where it will take you. Fighting change is like trying to struggle against a rip current in the ocean. The more you struggle, the further it pulls you out to sea.

Don't try to understand life either because it's far too complex for us to comprehend everything at once. That's why evolution is gradual, and we need to learn new things daily. Unfortunately, understanding everything can make you seem less natural too. Remember that flow is what you want.

Trust that the universe is guiding you. You might be religious, so use this to keep yourself grounded in knowing that there's something greater than you. You aren't thinking less of yourself, but you know that there's a universal purpose that's driving you towards a future that you'll appreciate more than what your heart desires now.

Also, stop overthinking everything and allow yourself to move in the direction that your creative genius is flowing. Whatever has happened is beyond change now. Maybe you messed up with your last book like the Mother Theresa book title incident. Keep reminding yourself that past failures don't define you.

Mindfulness and multitasking also make no sense together. Focus on one thing at a time and overcome it before stretching to another. Mental blocks won't be lifted if you're focused on 10 projects simultaneously. Give your full attention to a single desire and watch as it blossoms into an idea naturally.

Finally, let go of all the emotions and thoughts holding you back. Forget about the grudges you hold because they only harm you, whether it's towards other people or yourself. Let go of these emotions that dig their clutches deep into your creative splice. You can do this by meditating briefly throughout the day.

Daily Stress Meditations

Dissolve overwhelming feelings that flood you by applying a brief and personalized mediation session multiple times daily. Do it anywhere and at any time. Start by closing your eyes and allowing yourself to drop back into your body. Fear, stress, and overthinking can remove us from our present space in the body, and we must ground ourselves back into it. Allow the stress to show you where you physically feel pain, anguish, or fear. Give it a location in your body and simply notice it. Be with the physical sensations in your body for a moment and then move on to your mind.

Identify the ideals, narratives, and thoughts running amok. Recognize the reasons for the stress in your body. Allow them to manifest clear narratives and translate them to yourself. You're afraid because you hate changes. You're frightened by the unknown. You have this idea that the world should look a certain way, that you should be someone specific, and nothing looks the way it should. Notice the narrative that follows your thoughts. Are you judging yourself? Are you feeling ashamed or guilty? Listen to this narrative and acknowledge the truth.

It's only a familiar ideal you have of yourself. You think you need to look a certain way. You think you need to produce so much work in so much time. What about the alternatives? What if your mind wasn't limited to the ideals you have? Ideals are limitations you place on yourself, and they're malleable. You can change the ideals and voice a new narrative. That brings you to the final step of your mini-meditations. Intentionally let go of the stress from these narratives, ideals, thoughts and physical pains.

Allow yourself to fall back into the flow of life. Welcome the flow of creativity to change you into a better person than what you have in your mind. Your vision is limited, but the flow state provides unlimited possibilities. Just be who you are and accept your thoughts for being malleable. Let them go and commit yourself to be open to new ideas. You permit your thoughts to find their freedom. Be yourself and embark on the new journey life has to offer.

This is a sample of what you do in a mini-meditation. You can recognize any physical sensations within a minute and identify the thoughts that try to narrate your inner truth before accepting your true self as a malleable human who flows with life.

Letting Go for Optimal Creativeness

Learning to let go isn't as scary as it seems. It might be more enjoyable than you anticipate. There are four valuable ways of letting go to make sure you can release what needs to go.

The "Do Nothing" Approach

Writers commonly hit a block and find themselves lying on the couch and staring at the ceiling, often running their story through their minds. They weren't looking at the laptop but simply pondering the plot in their minds. In fact, an hour passed where they did nothing. Well, they've just had one of the most productive hours they'll ever experience. Their mind flowed into daydreaming where the plot came together while their eyes weren't glued to their screens. Sometimes, doing nothing is the most productive way to let go of block and allow ideas to come to you.

Even being bored can be productive, as crazy as that sounds. You can't force ideas to pop into your head while you stare at a blank canvas, but you can daydream while you're making dinner rather than stressing yourself out with the blank canvas. Doing nothing is like nurturing a different mindset where your imagination has the reins. So-called inactive brains are incubating spaces for the imagination. The world has become such a fast-paced rat race that we forget how to do nothing. We're always ticking our to-do lists and thinking about the next task while we're supposed to be focused on the task at hand.

Being too busy can work against your flow. It can actually be harmful. Professor Brian O'Conner from University College in Dublin says that we must embrace idleness before we crash and burn (Chabala, 2019). The fallacy we all believe in, where being busy as bees is always creatively productive, is merely a fallacy and nothing more. No one regrets not working harder in their old days. They regret not living more and experiencing great things that inspired them. Art and happiness are supposed to be intertwined and you can't be happy if you regret overworking yourself in later years.

The human body was only created to withstand so much, and pushing it past its limits isn't going to make you create art. You require a balance between doing nothing and working on your latest novel. Doing nothing all the time is more like being lazy though, so be careful not to tip your balance over the edge either. When you're ready, stop, slow down, and take a break. Doing nothing means no Netflix, Facebook, or scrolling through emails. It means that you must exert your energy in nothingness or at least in something other than using your mind. Hit the brakes and remove all distractions from the table.

Have you ever asked yourself why you switch Netflix on when you're bored? Most people are afraid of the chattering in their minds and don't want to face the thoughts bouncing about. However, creative people need this time because they must listen to the chatter. They must translate the ideas into a new meaning, and ultimately, art. Indeed, some people might lose their minds if they had to listen to the ideas in it, but you want to lose yourself in the ideas floating about your mind. Artists must become aware of what's going on in their minds so that they can create something new.

Honing your awareness and listening to that inner dialogue can be overwhelming at first, but it's how you switch your brain back to creativity. The default mode network (DMN) is what psychologists call this process. It's the process of listening to and questioning these ideas floating about to form new ideas. Meditation helps you reach the mindset needed to listen to your inner dialogue when you focus on your breathing and your inner voice. It's one method of tapping into the well of nothingness that overflows with brilliant ideas, but there are other ways to do it as well.

Become mindfully involved in routine activities that use the body and not your mind. For example, washing the dishes gives you a break. Coloring, knitting, and exercising also provide breaks from your unintentional force to be creative.

Partaking in other forms of art gives you an escape too, if you're fully engaged in them. Go to a concert, take a painting class if you're a writer, and listen to a poetry reading. Find new hobbies and treat them as hobbies. You aren't turning other creative avenues into new creative streams for yourself. You're simply relaxing the mind and body.

Just make sure you're keeping your balance strong. Don't forget to be creative when your mind is most energized, but allocate some breaks for times of the day you're feeling less energized. Always plan your breaks and work to make sure you aren't overusing the "do nothing" technique.

I recommend short bouts of doing nothing in between your work, as well. Don't work for five hours straight. Give yourself 10 minutes for every hour you work, and use this time to do nothing. You might even solve problems that were troubling you when you were working. Sitting in the garden has been a huge "do nothing" benefit for me. I've taken my 10-minute breaks and sat listening to the birds. Suddenly, I realize how I can fix something that wasn't flowing well in the chapter I just wrote.

Letting Go With Exercise

The connection between your creative self and your physical body is undeniable. Moving your body helps you to think better. A study in the Frontiers in Human Neuroscience Journal proved that moving our bodies makes our minds more creative (Gray, 2017). The participants who exercised four times weekly were far more creative in solving a series of tasks than their sedentary counterparts. They were able to think inside and outside of the box, and they came up with numerous ideas to solve the same problem. Even brief amounts of exercise can amplify your creative flow, and it gives you something to do when you need a break from your work.

More than 200 studies were included in Gray's report, and they all showed that long-term exercise fed the brain with chemicals that created the ultimate incubation stage for creative ideas. The type of exercise doesn't always matter, but aerobic exercises, such as dancing, swimming, and jogging showed significant improvements in their creative flow. Using low-impact exercise is also less daunting and helps keep your stress levels down. Running, walking, cycling, and any gentle form of aerobic exercise is the best. Another interesting find was that the creative boost from exercise is most significant for two hours after exercising.

There's nothing wrong with taking a Dictaphone on your walk or taking a camera along to snap inspirational images along the way. Exercise has also been shown to improve your ability to imagine new situations. Perhaps, it's because you're mindfully consuming inspiration as you walk through the park. It's also because the chemicals mentioned in Chapter Two multiply the pathways in the brain and strengthen the existing ones. You don't even have to think about creativeness while walking through the park. You simply need to be, and that's why exercise doubles as a "letting go" technique.

However, the secret is that it's most effective outdoors because nature is like a conductor that keeps our creativity flowing.

Letting Go in Nature

The University of Kansas studied the effects of nature on creativity (Inspire Portal, 2014). Participants spent a mere four days immersed in nature and disconnected from technology. Their performance, creativity, and problem-solving were boosted by an astronomical 50%. So, letting go by being immersed in nature is another way of overcoming mental block. Besides, nature is filled with inspiration beyond your wildest imagination. Your appreciation and awe are increased when you're engaged in it.

Nature can even improve your memory (Patel, 2017). You need a sharp memory to maintain a creative flow. It also feeds your body and mind with natural energy, boosting your depleted levels. The brain can then run on its highest analytical abilities when you spend 20 minutes daily in the beauty that is nature. And overall, the healthier your brain becomes, the better your mental state performs, meaning that depression, stress, and anxiety aren't as prevalent anymore.

Letting Go Socially

Spending time with loved ones, friends, and partners can help you let go of everything holding you back. Think of your time as a valuable commodity though, and choose who you spend it with wisely. Author Jim Rohn couldn't have said it better because we're the reflection of the five people we spend most of our time with (Drzymkowski, 2019). Remember that it's our second primal instinct to be social and leave our legacy behind. We need to leave some footprint in the sand of our community or family. Unfortunately, this can also be a bad thing. That's why you choose your "letting go" community wisely.

Your five closest people are the most influential on your attitude, mindset, and behavior. However, you can't go wrong if you're surrounded by people who encourage your positive and creative mindset. You want supportive people who don't judge you. You need a deeper bond with these people so that their influence can also permeate to your subconscious mind when you need to let go of worries, stress, and inevitable changes. Think about how you feel when you hug someone you truly care about. It doesn't only influence you, the closeness of positively supportive people can do much more.

The brain yearns for this as a primal need and it will release endorphins and oxytocin or love chemicals that strengthen the pathways even further. Sometimes, all we need is to be close to someone. So, going out with a good friend and having lunch with your sister are good options to break away and let go. Don't arrive with negative thoughts in your mind. Try to clear your mind and arrive with no intention of finding creative inspiration. It might come when you least expect it or your friend might give you the craziest idea, but you're only there to enjoy their company and chill.

Releasing the burdens of work and enjoying time with friends and family can be unintentionally, profoundly inspiring. At the end of the day, you can apply every command prompt, let go of concerns, and assert your title as an unstoppable creative genius, and it still won't happen. That's okay because you probably just need to de-stress first and relax. Don't blame yourself and don't start narrating untruths about false shortfalls. Sit back and allow inspiration to come to you again.

Conclusion

Creativity blooms in every light, under every rock, and in every person. You know how passionate you are, and you realize that no one has the right to hold you back, including yourself. A mental block is the enemy of creative genius. It stumps our rewards, and makes us wonder what the heck is wrong with us when we can't create what we want to. Staring at a screen, feeling lost when you look at a blank canvas, and feeling detached from your instrument when you're supposed to compose a new song is the inevitable journey every artist encounters.

How often have you hit a blank and couldn't piece together concepts to make an exquisite painting? The emotions that flood you at this point make you feel hopeless, angry, and fearful. You fear a future where your creativity has vanished forever. You're angry because you've created masterpieces in the past and now you can't write a single poem. You're disappointed because your music isn't touching souls as it used to.

Stop right now. End this emotional spiral that comes with the mental block every creative artist must endure. Beating yourself up about it certainly won't change your trajectory. It only makes you spiral deeper into the blockade in front of you. Clear your mind and take a breath before you kick yourself. Creativity is the most valuable skill to possess, but it feels like our hearts and guts are torn from us when it fails to ignite.

Creating art should be similar to easing your mind with suppressants, except you're using the natural flow of life to become so involved in your work and express every part of your heart and mind that you reach a new high. Creativity in its purest form is more than a career. Yes, it must gather value and provide an income to prove all the haters wrong, but its roots run far deeper than monetary rewards.

The ebb and flow of life connects with your creative genius, and then you'll find true fulfillment and actualization. Your work means more than dollars and cents to the observer. It speaks to them, without you voicing your expressions. Your music must drive their soul and your paintings must grab the core of their being. You're not only inspired by the world and all its glorious mentors, but you're also inspiring those around you.

Don't allow your creative side to become repressed by mental blocks, you have all the tricks, secrets, and techniques to open your expression to the world again so that they can say: "Wow, there are no words to describe the beauty I see." Make people see what they haven't seen before, and you'll be earning an income similar to my six-figure earnings. Motivation plays a role in creative genius, but it's much more than that.

Internal and external factors will either make you give up when you're blocked again, or it can be harnessed through simple techniques and practices to explode into an array of expressive, passionate, and rewarding work. You've learned all about the brain and how creativity is part of its daily functions. You know that mastering your unstoppable creativeness is as simple as owning your title and being true to yourself.

None of the world-famous artists became who they were by giving up. Picasso never stopped when he reached a mountain. No, he redesigned an abstract idea of the mountain and illustrated it for the world to see. Beethoven never allowed mental blocks to ravish his genius, and rather used the emotions inside of him to create music that resonated through to the deepest parts of the human soul.

Art is meaningful, deep, and emotional. It doesn't help if we allow our emotions, or those of the people around us, to squash our creative side when we reach an obstacle if emotions are the most powerful expression in creativity. Intelligence also plays a role but creation is driven by passion and desire, which are emotional factors. Intelligence is how you turn your emotional desires into an expression that makes people fall in love with it.

Keep pushing and asserting your inner child to make your work unstoppable, unmatchable, and beautiful enough to withstand any doubt, panic, or fear from your side or the judgmental observers. You know that their opinion matters as much as the Los Angeles Lakers defeating the Boston Celtics in the next showdown. The result of this match won't affect your life, and neither do other people's opinions.

The only people you want to impress are those who share your passion for art. You know how to advance your creative career now and avoid mental blocks from keeping you strapped to the hood of a car speeding towards a wall. Use the power of you, and tap into the intelligent creative in your mind to keep moving forward. Don't allow anyone to stop you from using your 20 tricks to be unstoppable.

You are what you choose to be and you've even learned to conduct the environment to match your artistry. Flow with life and allow it to flow inside of you with simple techniques that create an environment conducive to spontaneous and masterful ingenuity. Breaking through a mental block can be as simple as applying the 20 secrets I've shared with you to ensure creation on command.

And finally, you know when to let go and allow your art to create itself in your busy mind. Creative geniuses have something in common. We always find a way to overcome the block because there's no one as ingenious as an unstoppable creative. We find answers that other people overlook. We surf inspiration that hides from creatively blind individuals. We use all the ideas that other people failed at, and create something that works.

Nothing stands between you and your creative edge anymore. You have every trick that works and you know how to remove the background noise when it overwhelms you. The only thing standing in your way now is the self-doubt. Use the methods laid out to overcome self-doubt and spread your wings as wide as you can. You are anyone your heart desires, and you can create a showstopper.

Go out there and be the greatest name to embrace this generation.

References

Aayad, F. (2017, May 10). *This is what 'letting go' really means because it's more than moving on.* Thought Catalog. https://thoughtcatalog.com/farah-ayaad/2017/05/this-is-what-letting-go-really-means-because-its-more-than-moving-on/

Agrawal, A. J. (2015, March 18). *4 reasons you should never stop learning.* Inc.com. https://www.inc.com/aj-agrawal/4-reasons-why-we-should-never-stop-learning.html#:~:text=Self%2Dgrowth%20is%20key%20to

Allan, P. (2014, October 4). *How being humble, kind, and calm will make your life easier.* Lifehacker. https://lifehacker.com/how-being-humble-kind-and-calm-will-make-your-life-ea-1561763720

Alnuweiri, T. (2018, February 26). *What you eat could impact your creativity.* Well and Good. https://www.wellandgood.com/gut-health-diet-increases-creativity/

Athuraliya, A. (2019, October 10). *How to write an action plan | step-by-step guide with templates.* Creately Blog.

https://creately.com/blog/diagrams/how-to-write-an-action-plan/

Babauta, L. (n.d.-a). *9 steps to achieving flow (and happiness) in your work*. Zen Habits. https://zenhabits.net/guide-to-achieving-flow-and-happiness-in-your-work/

Babauta, L. (n.d.-b). *A guide to letting go of stress*. Zen Habits. https://zenhabits.net/stress-guide/

Bardsley, A. (2018, November 2). *How your surroundings affect your wellbeing*. Thrive Global. https://thriveglobal.com/stories/how-your-surroundings-affect-your-wellbeing/

Barratt, E. L., & Davis, N. J. (2015). Autonomous sensory meridian response (ASMR): a flow-like mental state. *PeerJ*, 3, e851. https://doi.org/10.7717/peerj.851

Bauce. (2019, June 3). *How to tap into the power of being your authentic self*. Bauce. https://baucemag.com/power-of-being-your-authentic-self/

Beard, C. (2019, February 10). *How to design an action plan for your goals*. The Blissful Mind. https://theblissfulmind.com/action-steps-for-goals/

Benve, R. (2020, August 11). *10 tips to get over a creativity burnout and boost artistic inspiration*. Felt Magnet.

https://feltmagnet.com/artist-corner/how-to-find-artistic-inspiration

Booth, J. (2018, January 9). *8 ways to trick yourself into feeling confident, even when you're not.* Insider. https://www.insider.com/how-to-be-more-confident-2018-1

Brown, L. (2018, February 5). *10 mindful attitudes to help overcome anxiety.* Hack Spirit. https://hackspirit.com/10-mindful-attitudes-rewire-brain-let-go-anxiety/

Brownson, T. (2015, September 14). *If you want to be creative, stop trying to be creative.* A Daring Adventure. https://adaringadventure.com/if-you-want-to-be-creative-stop-trying-to-be-creative/

Cavdarbasha, D., & Kurczek, J. (2017). Connecting the dots: Your brain and creativity. *Frontiers for Young Minds, 5.* https://doi.org/10.3389/frym.2017.00019

Chabala, T. (2019, December 6). *Why doing nothing is actually one of the best things you can do.* Shondaland. https://www.shondaland.com/live/body/a301 25041/why-doing-nothing-is-actually-one-of-the-best-things-you-can-do/

Cho, A. (2015, June 23). *Some basic principles of Feng Shui.* The Spruce. https://www.thespruce.com/what-is-feng-shui-1275060

Creative Living Works. (n.d.-a). *Feng Shui your creative space.* Creative Living Works. https://creativelivingworks.com/posts/feng-shui.php

Csikszentmihalyi, M. (2016). *Flow, the secret to happiness.* Ted Talk. https://www.ted.com/talks/mihaly_csikszentmihalyi_flow_the_secret_to_happiness

Dienstman, A. M. (2020, May 13). *Feng Shui can help you rediscover passion & creativity indoors.* Good Net. https://www.goodnet.org/articles/feng-shui-help-you-rediscover-passion-creativity-indoors

DiMaria, F. (2015, June 16). *Is the "app mentality" killing students' creativity?* The Journal. https://thejournal.com/Articles/2015/06/16/Is-the-App-Mentality-Killing-Students-Creativity

DiSalvo, D. (2013, March 26). *10 reasons why we struggle with creativity.* Psychology Today. https://www.psychologytoday.com/us/blog/neuronarrative/201303/10-reasons-why-we-struggle-creativity

Dooley, R. (2016, July 22). *Forget plan B -- science says you should be all in.* Forbes. https://www.forbes.com/sites/rogerdooley/2016/07/22/forget-plan-b/#35ded2c0275e

Drzymkowski, B. (2019, December 23). *Spending time with loved ones reduces stress.* Medium.

https://medium.com/@brandy.drz/spending-time-with-loved-ones-reduces-stress-fc370c2b6272

Dummies. (n.d.-b). *Mindfulness and the psychology of flow.* Dummies. https://www.dummies.com/religion/spiritualit y/mindfulness-and-the-psychology-of-flow/

Eby, D. (2020, August 30). *Highly sensitive people: Latent inhibition and creativity.* Highly Sensitive and Creative. http://highlysensitive.org/64/highly-sensitive-people-latent-inhibition-and-creativity/

Emmer, J. (2018). *What is Feng Shui? A brief history of Feng Shui.* Feng Shui Style. http://fengshuistyle.us/what-is-feng-shui/history/

Exploring Your Mind. (2019a, January 15). *Normopathy: Know the desire to be like others.* Exploring Your Mind. https://exploringyourmind.com/normopathy-unhealthy-desire-everyone-else/

Fishbein, R. (n.d.). *How not to care when people don't like you.* Pocket. https://getpocket.com/explore/item/how-not-to-care-when-people-don-t-like-you

Gates, A. (2015, May 1). *How to boost your creativity with Feng Shui.* Amanda Gates Feng Shui.

https://gatesinteriordesign.com/how-to-boost-
your-creativity-with-feng-shui/

Giardina, R. (2019, August 19). *What is the cost of
withholding your truth?* InnerSelf.
https://innerself.com/content/personal/attitud
es-transformed/fear-and-worry/4310-always-
tell-your-truth.html

Gray, M. (2017, February 23). *How exercise is good for
increasing creativity.* Irish Mental Health Charity in
Ireland.
https://www.alustforlife.com/tools/how-
exercise-is-good-for-increasing-creativity

Hammond, R. (2016, July 29). *Where does creativity come
from?* Engadget.
https://www.engadget.com/2016-07-29-where-
does-creativity-come-
from.html#:~:text=Creativity%20comes%20an
ytime%20we%20need

Hardy, B. (2017, January 6). *30 behaviors of unstoppable
people.* Inc. https://www.inc.com/benjamin-p-
hardy/30-behaviors-that-will-make-you-
unstoppable.html

Headspace. (2019b). *What is a flow state and what are its
benefits?* Headspace.
https://www.headspace.com/articles/flow-
state

Hellwig, P. (2018, August 14). *The importance of finding and standing in our truth.* Tiny Buddha. https://tinybuddha.com/blog/the-importance-of-finding-and-standing-in-our-truth/

Herring, A. (2017, August 22). *Six ways to find creative inspiration (when you're just not feeling it).* Pace. https://www.paceco.com/insights/design-development/six-ways-find-creative-inspiration/

Hertzberg, K. (2017, January 9). *21 ways to inspire creativity when you're out of ideas.* Grammarly. https://www.grammarly.com/blog/ways-to-inspire-creativity/

Ho, L. (2006, January 27). *How to plan your life goals and actually achieve them in 7 simple steps.* Lifehack. https://www.lifehack.org/articles/lifehack/9-steps-to-define-your-goal-destination-and-devise-a-plan-to-get-there.html

Hoge, E. A., Bui, E., Marques, L., Metcalf, C. A., Morris, L. K., Robinaugh, D. J., Worthington, J. J., Pollack, M. H., & Simon, N. M. (2013). Randomized controlled trial of mindfulness meditation for generalized anxiety disorder. *The Journal of Clinical Psychiatry,* 74(08), 786–792. https://doi.org/10.4088/jcp.12m08083

Inspire Portal. (2014, May 19). *Awakening your creativity through nature: 10 creative benefits of spending time in nature.* Inspire Portal.

http://inspireportal.com/awakening-your-creativity-through-nature/#:~:text=A%20study%20conducted%20by%20the

Jari Roomer. (2019, February 12). *How to reach flow state (using 10 flow state 'triggers')*. Medium. https://medium.com/personal-growth-lab/how-to-reach-flow-state-using-10-flow-state-triggers-473aa28dc3e5

John, J. (2019, October 29). *In an age of fasts, microdosing and hyper-productivity, it's vital we understand how lack of sleep can affect a creative mind*. We Heart. https://www.we-heart.com/2019/10/29/how-lack-of-sleep-affects-a-creative-mind/#:~:text=Disrupted%20REM%20sleep%20can%20slow

Kayte. (2020, January 20). *10 reasons why you should never stop learning*. Enjoying the Art of Living. https://www.enjoyingtheartofliving.com/10-reasons-why-you-should-never-stop-learning/

Kennedy, A. (2016, April 5). *Flow state: What it is and how to achieve it*. HuffPost. https://www.huffpost.com/entry/flow-state-what-it-is-and_b_9607084?guccounter=1

Kreitzer, M. J., Zborowsky, T., & Larson, J. (2016). *What impact does the environment have on us?* Taking Charge. https://www.takingcharge.csh.umn.edu/what-

impact-does-environment-have-
us#:~:text=The%20environment%20can%20in
fluence%20peoples

Kwik, J. (2020, April 10). *Create a designated work space—
your brain needs it.* Medium.
https://medium.com/@kwikbrain/create-a-
designated-work-space-your-brain-needs-it-
bf1e9ae25f1b#:~:text=Creating%20our%20ow
n%20space%20is%20vital%20when%20workin
g%20from%20home.&text=And%20while%20
we

Lobell, K. O. (2018, August 21). *What is creativity?
Defining the skill of the future.* Creative Live Blog.
https://www.creativelive.com/blog/what-is-
creativity/

Logue, G. (2016, August 22). *Finding inspiration in those
around you.* Medium.
https://blog.buckets.co/finding-inspiration-in-
those-around-you-54fbeb20a688

Loria, K. (2016, November 4). *Exercise might be more than
good for your brain — it could make you more creative
as well.* Business Insider.
https://www.businessinsider.com/exercise-
benefits-brain-creativity-stress-2016-11?IR=T

Luke, A. (2019, April 15). *Why doing nothing is more
productive than you might think.* Craft Your
Content.

https://www.craftyourcontent.com/productive
-doing-nothing/

Luna, A. (2017, September 11). *9 exhilarating ways to be true to yourself (even when you're scared)*. LonerWolf. https://lonerwolf.com/be-true-to-yourself/

Madill, E. (2018, January 24). *How to stay standing in your truth around difficult people and circumstances*. Emily Madill. https://emilymadill.com/stay-standing-truth-around-difficult-people-circumstance/

Malarcher, P. (2012, August 31). **Feng Shui* your studio to maximize creative flow*. Surface Design Association. https://www.surfacedesign.org/feng-shui-your-studio-to-maximize-creative-flow/

Maros, M. (2019, June 16). *Honoring your desires*. Peaceful Mind Peaceful Life. https://peacefulmindpeacefullife.org/honoring-your-desires/

Matyszczyk, C. (2016, August 21). *You have a plan B? Science says that's a really bad idea*. Inc. https://www.inc.com/chris-matyszczyk/you-have-a-plan-b-science-says-thats-a-really-bad-idea.html

Metcalf, M. (2019, September 5). *In the flow: How to master your brain's peak productivity*. Trello Blog. https://blog.trello.com/brain-flow-state

Moore, C. (2019, May 27). *How to set and achieve life goals the right way.* Positive Psychology. https://positivepsychology.com/life-worth-living-setting-life-goals/

Mott, R. (2018, January 28). *10 signs that you are not standing in your truth, loving yourself, and living your unique and….* Medium. https://medium.com/@rebeccahmott/let-your-authenticity-and-love-of-your-unique-style-be-your-guide-to-who-you-truly-are-9a576bb8fc1e

Nakamura, J., & Csikszentmihalyi, M. (2009). Flow theory and research. *The Oxford Handbook of Positive Psychology*, 194–206. https://doi.org/10.1093/oxfordhb/978019518 7243.013.0018

NASAA. (2015). *Facts & figures on the creative economy.* NASAA. https://nasaa-arts.org/nasaa_research/facts-figures-on-the-creative-economy/

Newman, T. (2016, February 17). *The neuroscience of creativity.* Medical News Today. https://www.medicalnewstoday.com/articles/3 06611

Nielson, D. (n.d.). Nothing is truly original: What nobody told you about being creative. *The Journal of Healthcare Contracting.* https://www.jhconline.com/nothing-is-truly-original-what-nobody-told-you-about-being-creative.html

Patel, D. (2017, April 20). *5 ways spending time in nature enhances creativity.* Medium. https://medium.com/thrive-global/nature-inspires-creativity-66254fe3d537

Patricia, & Azlin. (2018, July 26). *Running out of creative juices? Drink more water!* Pat-Lin. https://patlin.com.my/2018/07/26/running-out-of-creative-juices-drink-more-water/#:~:text=Benefits%20of%20water&text=Water%20is%20vital%20not%20only

Psychology Wiki. (n.d.-c). *Latent inhibition.* Psychology Wiki. https://psychology.wikia.org/wiki/Latent_inhibition

Quy, L. (2016, July 8). *7 mental hacks to be more confident in yourself.* Success. https://www.success.com/7-mental-hacks-to-be-more-confident-in-yourself/

Rankin, L. (n.d.). *How to honor your desires without grasping, denying, or bypassing.* Lissa Rankin. https://lissarankin.com/how-to-honor-your-desires-without-grasping-denying-or-bypassing/

Sapiurka, M. (2015, October 18). *Coming up blank: the science of writer's block.* The Conversation.

https://theconversation.com/coming-up-blank-the-science-of-writers-block-47853

Singer, A. (2010, February 26). *Trying too hard may be the reason for your failure.* The Future Buzz. https://thefuturebuzz.com/2010/02/26/trying-too-hard/

The Money Chat. (2015, December 30). *The importance of having a dedicated workspace at home.* Money Chat. https://www.themoneychat.com/importance-dedicated-workspace-home/

Tillman, T. (2018, September 16). *How do you get in touch with your true self?* InnerSelf. https://innerself.com/content/personal/happiness-and-self-help/self-help/9861-getting-in-touch-with-your-true-self.html

Tong, L. (2016, July 6). *10 surprising reasons to stop trying to please everyone.* Tiny Buddha. https://tinybuddha.com/blog/10-surprising-reasons-stop-trying-please-everyone/

Ulrich, R., Quan, X., Zimring, C., Joseph, A., & Choudhary, R. (2004). *The role of the physical environment in the hospital of the 21 st century: A once-in-a-lifetime opportunity.* Health Design. https://www.healthdesign.org/sites/default/files/Role%20Physical%20Environ%20in%20the%2021st%20Century%20Hospital_0.pdf

Wharton, L. (2014, August 5). *Why Letting Go Could Kick-Start Your Creativity.* Distilled. https://www.distilled.net/resources/why-letting-go-could-kick-start-your-creativity/

Wiggins, G. A., Tyack, P., Scharff, C., & Rohrmeier, M. (2015). The evolutionary roots of creativity: Mechanisms and motivations. *Philosophical Transactions of the Royal Society B: Biological Sciences*, 370(1664), 20140099. https://doi.org/10.1098/rstb.2014.0099

WikiHow. (2019c, May 27). *How to find creative inspiration.* WikiHow. https://www.wikihow.com/Find-Creative-Inspiration

Zaidel, D. W. (2014). Creativity, brain, and art: Biological and neurological considerations. *Frontiers in Human Neuroscience*, 8. https://doi.org/10.3389/fnhum.2014.00389

Zakrzewski, V. (2016, January 12). *How humility will make you the greatest person ever.* Greater Good - Berkeley Education. https://greatergood.berkeley.edu/article/item/humility_will_make_you_greatest_person_ever#:~:text=For%20example%2C%20humble%20people%20handle,draw%20us%20closer%20to%20others

Made in the USA
Monee, IL
15 November 2020

47839552R00095